The Global Financial Challenges of Entrepreneurship, E-Commerce, Terrorism and COVID-19

The Global Financial Challenges of Entrepreneurship, E-Commerce, Terrorism and COVID-19

By

Kiran Javaria and Omar Masood

Cambridge
Scholars
Publishing

The Global Financial Challenges of Entrepreneurship, E-Commerce, Terrorism and COVID-19

By Kiran Javaria and Omar Masood

This book first published 2023

Cambridge Scholars Publishing

Lady Stephenson Library, Newcastle upon Tyne, NE6 2PA, UK

British Library Cataloguing in Publication Data
A catalogue record for this book is available from the British Library

ISBN (10): 1-5275-1013-1
ISBN (13): 978-1-5275-1013-5

TABLE OF CONTENTS

PREFACE

Global financial management determines the health and performance of the world economy. While a global pandemic has been a looming risk for decades, Covid-19 has come as a shock to society, health systems, economies and governments worldwide. Whenever there is a recession or economic slowdown Governments try to lift economic confidence with stimulus of different kinds. The Covid-19 Pandemic is a one-of-a-kind health and economic incident during the last century. One of the reasons for this immediate and timely stimulus is governments did not want this slowdown cycle to convert into a full economic depression where it is very hard to control prices going down. If we look the world economy after the great recession it was not able to fully recover by the time of Covid-19's beginning, due to which it was a more difficult task for the governments and central banks of the world economies and especially the developed world to contain the Covid shock. Therefore, governments and central banks tried their best to use whatever tools they had in their arsenal and to use them fully.

The biggest opportunity presented by Covid-19 is the chance to reset some of our economic approaches in a way that maximizes the chances of developing more resilient and sustainable approaches to globalization. Innovation, adaptation and entrepreneurial spirit are particularly important when dealing with global challenges that threaten everyone, like pandemics and climate change. Covid-19 has produced uncertainty within the financial sector for both businesses making money and individuals taking care of their money. Prudent financial management now seems to be more important than ever, in addition to planning for the unthinkable, where institutions, firms and individuals all are insuring themselves against possible losses. This book highlights these strategists through a series of chapters.

This book is designed for anyone who is interested in understanding current global financial challenges which are affecting everyone due to the Covid-19 pandemic. The core objective of this book is to bring together different factors which are influencing our financial markets like entrepreneurship, e-commerce and terrorism how they are influencing our financial decisions.

This book is designed for learners from the fields of economics, finance, accounting and financial management, highlighting the most important and relevant topics. Students and teachers from universities all over the world including the UK, the USA, India, Pakistan, Canada, Australia, and Malaysia among others will enhance their abilities and understanding of these most pertinent issues. Every chapter in this book is very relevant and equipped with most up-to-date figures, tables, and charts. The book's material is globally relevant, rather than being relevant only to a specific region.

This book not only identifies these new challenges but provides future recommendations and strategies to mitigate these financial risks. This book is a must-read for professionals, bankers, students of business and finance and policy makers.

INTRODUCTION

Innovation, adaptation and entrepreneurial spirit are particularly important when dealing with global challenges that threaten everyone, like pandemics, terrorism and climate change.

The **first chapter** of this book explains the management of legal risk in e-commerce during the Covid time period. This chapter explains the different barriers faced by financial managers during the uncertain and legally risky situation created by the coronavirus. This chapter provides a major contribution to the e-commerce technology world as it explains the concept of legal risk in marketing in the e-commerce world as there is currently insufficient research on the concept despite its critical importance in influencing the behaviour of consumers.

Chapter two focuses on the "Global Fear and Uncertainty" effect of the Coronavirus crisis (USCovid-19), the fear index, and oil price in the United States' equity market. This is the first time the novel proxy of the fear index (Infectious Disease EMV index), developed by Baker et al. (2020), has been used. The study collected the data from 21 January 2020 which was the start of novel coronavirus (Covid-19) in America (US) up till August (2020). This ground-breaking insight is beneficial for individuals, researchers and policy makers world-wide.

The aim of the **third chapter** is to investigate the impact of oil prices on the stock markets of G7 countries. Oil prices not only affect the economy of a country but also the country's stock market. The stock market is essentially directly connected to the stock valuation whereas the stock value is associated with a discounted sum of predictable future cash flows and these flows may be distressed due to macroeconomic variables in the shape of oil price fluctuations during stressful times.

The **fourth chapter** introduces the concept of technology entrepreneurship which is the engine of growth in emerging economies after Covid-19. Entrepreneurship education has been characterized as an essential driver of sustainable socio-economic development as it plays a significant role in performing productive activities efficiently and effectively by using commitments, initiatives and innovative efforts.

The **fifth chapter** highlights the uncertainty and financial risk faced by international financial institutions and how this impacts the profitability and liquidity of banks in Europe. This chapter used various financial performance ratios of 100 banks operating in different European countries over five-year period (2011 to 2015) to investigate if such a relationship exists.

The **sixth chapter** introduces the global challenges of Enterprise Risk Management. The arrival of ERM is a natural evolution of risk management, so that risks can be managed at an organization-wide level. Enterprise Risk Management is an invention of this century and it has emerged mainly as an approach which addresses the limitations of Traditional Risk Management. No doubt, it's a supreme subject, especially for those firms which have a desire for success in the future. Since its commencement, it has turned into a standard instrument to manage the diversified risks of organization, dealing the operational as well as strategic risks, and transforming the risks into opportunities.

Seven chapter explains the impact of terrorism activities on different economies' (Developing and Developed) financial stock markets. Spain, the United Kingdom, India, Pakistan, America and France were chosen for analysis. The variables considered were terrorist activities and the market return of the stock markets. The results suggest that the market return is affected by terror events and the model is statistically significant.

The eighth chapter of the book discusses the increasing trust in e-commerce during the Covid-19 pandemic. The explosion of e-commerce activities required academia and industry to recognize the key factors of customer online repurchase intention. The purpose of writing this chapter was to determine the primary drivers of customer repeat-purchase intention. Online shopper repeat purchase intention is affected by many factors like consumer inertia and online trust. Managers and academics know fairly little about how the collective effect of consumer inertia and online trust on repeat-purchase intention.

CHAPTER 1

ISSUES AND CHALLENGES IN IMPLEMENTING E-COMMERCE DURING COVID TIMES

Summary of Chapter One

This chapter explains the management of legal risk in e-commerce during the Covid-19 time period. The problem statement/purpose of this chapter is to explain what the different barriers faced by financial managers during the uncertain and legally risky situation of coronavirus are. This chapter provides a major contribution in the technological e-commerce world. This is a very important topic as it explains the concept of legal risk in e-commerce marketing, as there is currently insufficient research on the concept, despite its critical importance in influencing the behavior of consumers. It utilizes both primary and secondary data from Gulf Cooperation Council (GCC) countries in order to get reliable results. There are different risk factors that affect the purchasing behavior of consumers who shop online. The consumer's perception of risk during Covid-19 times may be the result of all the emotional processes through which consumers recognize, organize, and provide meaning to the sensations felt, such as the need for product quality, online safety, and overall satisfaction. The primary data consists of a survey of online shoppers. The data and questionnaire was administered to 972 GCC internet users, who were classed as experienced and avid users between 2019 and 2021. The secondary data includes an analysis of the various theories of consumer behavior, models of online adoption, legal risk factors to marketing and shopping online, models of the adoption of innovation, and new ways of marketing and trade. Both techniques are utilized to examine the relationship between perceived risk strategies and customer satisfaction, as well as examining customer involvement and the propensity to take risks within existing relations of online shopping.

Keywords: E-Commerce, Risk Management, Financial Manager, Perceived Risk Strategies, Customer Satisfaction, Customer Involvement, Propensity to Take Risk, Covid-19

Section 1: Introduction

In today's competitive environment, technology is the most efficient means through which organizations communicate, keep themselves in touch with markets, and gain competitive advantage. This chapter will discuss how the Covid-19 crisis is accelerating an expansion of e-commerce within organizations, customers, and types of product, which is likely to involve a long-term shift of e-commerce transactions from luxury goods and services to everyday necessities. E-commerce shopping, or buying through the internet, is a rapidly growing phenomena (Lim, Osman· et al. 2016) especially during Covid-19 times. It is important for e-retailers to maintain customer re-purchase intentions and sustain operations in order to gain competitive advantage in the market (Kuo, Hu & Yang 2013). In an e-commerce world, it is important for service providers to engage with customers and provide them with security against all the risks faced by online consumers. Kim & Hong (2010) and Cunningham et al. (2005) examined the impact on the adoption of purchasing through the internet, and have outlined the risks as: financial, functional, social, and the physical environment, incorporating the fifth dimension of this specific sales system, and the risk of privacy. Kim et al. (2005) contrast the opposite effect, by detecting significant dimensions of risk on purchase intention via the internet, but not attitudes toward such behavior. Based on the work of Gierl et al. (2003) the effect of six dimensions of perceived risk on the adoption of electronic commerce was analyzed. In particular, these authors refer to functional components, financial, time, psychological, and social risk, and privacy, arguing that the last replaces the physical risk in the electronic environment. The empirical evidence supports the influence gained in all dimensions, except the social intentions of the adoption of electronic commerce (Bianchi & Mathews 2016).

The motivation behind writing this chapter is that it strongly contributes to the available research materials on marketing risk in Covid-19 times. Despite the quantity of published studies on the subject, including several reviews (Mitchell et al. 1990, Laroche et al. 2004), most of the research in this area focuses on the perception of risk in relation to product categories, disregarding the means to purchase and customer satisfaction. This chapter provides a major contribution to the e-commerce technology world. The aim of the chapter is to study the concept of risk in e-commerce marketing as there is currently insufficient research into the concept, despite its critical importance in influencing the behavior of consumers. The analysis of risk has not been limited to academic boundaries; it has been investigated in areas such medicine and social sciences, among others (Klein, Sterk 2003). It is stated by many authors that e-commerce shopping is one of the most rapid growing phenomena nowadays (Lim, Osman· et al. 2016). This area of knowledge has a great influence on theories of marketing, especially in the analysis of consumer behavior. The aim of the study is to identify the different theories and dimensions of risk by consumers as they purchase through e-commerce, analyze the efforts of the consumer through the strategies of reducing legal risk in the process of purchase through e-commerce, and measure consumer satisfaction in the process of buying.

The main contribution of this chapter is to identify the best practice lessons and legal principles in Gulf Cooperation Council (GCC) countries for e-commerce businesses during crisis times such as during the Covid-19 pandemic. One of the main objectives of the GCC is to achieve consistency and harmonization in the legislative frameworks of the Gulf States, especially in the area of e-commerce, which covers local and cross-border sales of goods and services via electronic means. This makes it a particularly interesting legal study for investigating the extent to which developing legislation in electronic contract law and e-commerce can be said to contribute to the level of prosperity and the growth of e-commerce within a selected region of GCC countries.

This chapter is divided into four parts. The second part will provide a critical analysis which explains different types of risk reduction strategies and their impact on customer satisfaction during Covid-19, and also supports this with the theoretical background. The third part demonstrates the measures used to justify the methodology of the paper. The fourth part will present empirical statistics, and the fifth part will conclude with recommendations.

Section 2: Critical analysis on risk reduction strategies

a) E-commerce legal regulations

A number of federal, state, and international laws now govern e-commerce, which can involve complex contract and tax issues, and security, and privacy concerns. Because technology changes quickly, the laws regulating it are new and developing. The Uniform Computer Information Transactions Act (UCITA) intends to bring uniformity and certainty to the laws that apply to information technology transactions, just as the Uniform Commercial Code does for the sale of goods (Nasir 2004). A few e-commerce laws of GCC countries are mentioned in Appendix (A).

b) The Global and National Commerce Acts (E-SIGN Act)

There are a few Global and National Commerce Acts, which are enforced in various countries. The E-SIGN Act defines the 'electronic signature' (sometimes called a 'digital signature') as an electronic sound, symbol, or process, attached to, or logically associated with, a contract or other record, and executed or adopted by a person with the intent to sign the record. Because of this broad definition, telephone keypad agreements, (such as 'press 1 to agree') may be legally enforced as electronic contracts under the Act. A contract may not be denied legal effect just because a digital signature was used to form it. The E-SIGN Act, which regulates any transactions in interstate and foreign commerce, does not alter existing law, and if state or federal law, including the Uniform Commercial Code, covers a transaction, those statutes supersede (Peter & Deveaux 2000).

c) Legal action for data protection and privacy violations

Privacy is one of the most complex legal issues facing e-commerce today. Many sites collect personal information about their users, including names, addresses, and credit card information. Consumers who have pursued legal action because of privacy violations, including breach of contract, unjust enrichment, fraud, and trespass to chattels, or have invoked state statutes prohibiting deceptive or unfair trade practices by businesses, have successfully used common law to obtain redress. Some state laws specifically protect particular classes of data, such as medical information. The Federal Trade Commission (FTC) has recommended legislation to regulate online profiling. The FTC has used its authority to sue corporations that do not comply with privacy policies posted on their websites (Barr & David 2000).

d) Copyright and trademark

Many attempts have been made to address the issues related to copyright of digital content. E-commerce has a tremendous impact on copyright and related issues, and the scope of copyright is affecting how e-commerce evolves. It is essential that legal rules are set and applied appropriately to ensure that digital technology does not undermine the basic doctrine of copyright and related rights. From one perspective, the internet has been described as the world's biggest copy machine. Older technologies such as photocopying, recording and taping are bound by rules and regulations regarding quantity, content, quality, and time constraints. In contrast, on the internet, one person can send millions of copies all over the world (Robert and Thomas 2000)

e) Theoretical Background

In the theory "Effort in Purchase" proposed by Laroche et al. (2004), it is suggested that the greater the effort made by the consumer in a particular purchase, the greater will be the perception of satisfaction with the purchase process. Thus, the perception of the outcome of the bid would be shaped in accordance with the effort invested (Sobihah et al. 2015). This theory supports this study and explains that individuals tend to perceive a measure of satisfaction as a result of effort expended in the pursuit of an item. It emphasizes that the degree of involvement with the purchase has an influence on the risk perceived by consumers and reduction strategies (Dholakia 1997) leading to the perception of satisfaction with the purchase process. Many studies have been conducted on consumer online purchasing (McCole et al. 2010). Each consumer purchasing a product, or different products, in different situations, may have a greater or lesser perception of risk (Park, Bhatnagar & Rao 2010).

f) Relationship analysis

i) The effect of legal risk in online marketing on consumer purchase satisfaction

Evidence supporting the influence of risk on the behavior of consumers who shop online has been highlighted by numerous authors in the field. The attitude of online buyers significantly and positively affects customers' satisfaction and their online purchasing behavior. The management of consumers' risk is very important in their internet-based transactions. Sobihah et al. (2015) analyzed the effect of uncertainty about the product (risk functional) and the shipping process (source of risk) on the adoption of trade. For its part, the empirical evidence obtained by Lim (2003) observed that the guarantees of privacy positively affect confidence in purchasing on the web, and through its intended behavior (Choi, Kim & Kim 2011). There are various types of risk which are defined respectively as follows:

Legal and financial risk: Pires et al. (2004) state that legal and financial risk is employed in studies that relate to the potential loss of economic capital by the consumer, or to the purchase and/or use of the product or service purchased (Mercado & Rajagopal 2015). This is the risk that the product is not worth the cost (Schiffman, Kanuk 1997), and in a broader definition, the financial risk is any risk related to loss of property and money (Solomon 1998).

Risk of performance and risk functional: Bateson and Hoffman (2001) explain the concept that the product or service purchased may not correspond to the task for which it was purchased. The risk functional, or performance, is risk that the product does not have the expected performance. It can be mitigated through customer satisfaction (Sobihah et al. 2015).

ii) Risk mitigation strategies in online electronic commerce:

There are various strategies which organizations can use to minimize the risks of online electronic commerce (Lim, Osman· et al. 2016). These strategies are given below:

Online networking: A strategy to reduce the risk perceived by the search for information. This is that the risk can be minimized through online networking sites, which lots of consumers subscribe to, where information is shared on product reviews (Kim 2005). The benefit of this is that the network provides reviews of customers around the world, online, quickly, and without cost. (Kuo, Hu & Yang 2013).

Search for online reviewers and rating systems: In a study conducted by Wu et al. (2004), the results indicate that major strategies for risk reduction, with regard to high ratings of the product purchased are: firstly the group of reference (except for products of high perceived risk, which would feature an image or standards mark), followed by the retailer's reputation, the brand image, and guarantees (Lim, Osman· et al. 2016).

iii) The involvement of the consumer and the propensity to take risk (as a moderator):

One of the aspects mentioned in the literature of consumer behavior is influences on purchasing decisions and the individual's involvement with the process, product, and brand (Solomon 2002). The consumer's involvement is defined as the perceived relevance of an individual to an object based on their needs, values, and interests (Ranaweera 2016). Corroborating this idea, Engel et al. (1995) comment that this involvement increases when social pressure is perceived, i.e. the extent to which consumers feel they will be judged by an acquisition (Sobihah et al. 2015).

The involvement can be seen as the motivation to process information, in that, where there is a connection between the perceived needs, goals or values of, and knowledge of a consumer product, the individual will be motivated to pay attention to information about it (Mou, Shin, Cohen 2015).

iv) Cross-border law enforcement

Cross-border law enforcement can be defined as imposing sanctions on a business in state other than the one in which the law enforcer is established. It is assumed that the sanction is imposed due to the infringement of the law of the state in which the law enforcer is established, and that that law is different from the law in the state where the business is established. This article contains a division between traditional law enforcement (direct law enforcement) and alternative law enforcement (indirect law enforcement). Traditional law enforcement is sanctions imposed on the primary offender (the business) through the Judiciary, whereas alternative law enforcement comprises other sanctions, such as imposing joint liability on intermediaries (secondary offenders), employing technical measures, or using market forces (Singh 2018).

Figure 1: Theoretical framework

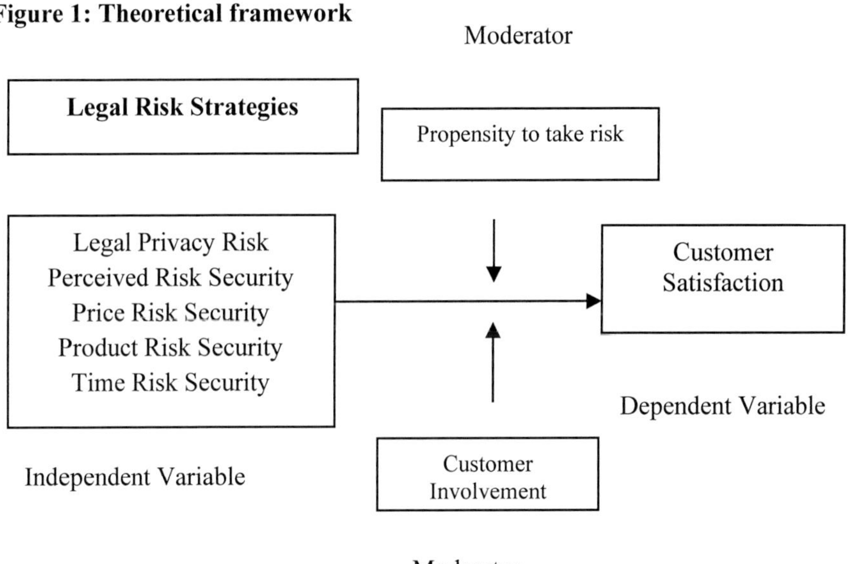

Hypothesis development:

H1: The legal risk reduction strategies have significant and positive impact on customer satisfaction in e-commerce during Covid-19.

H1a: The perceived risk strategies have significant and positive impact on customer satisfaction in e-commerce.

H1b: The price risk strategies have significant and positive impact on customer satisfaction in e-commerce.

H1c: The product risk strategies have significant and positive impact on customer satisfaction in e-commerce.

H1d: The legal privacy risk strategies have significant and positive impact on customer satisfaction in e-commerce.

H1e: The time risk strategies have significant and positive impact on customer satisfaction in e-commerce.

H2: The involvement moderates the relationship between legal risk reduction strategies and customer satisfaction in e-commerce during Covid-19.

H2a: The involvement moderates the relationship between perceived risk strategies and customer satisfaction in e-commerce.

H2b: The involvement moderates the relationship between price risk strategies and customer satisfaction in e-commerce.

H2c: The involvement moderates the relationship between product risk strategies and customer satisfaction in e-commerce.

H2d: The involvement moderates the relationship between legal privacy risk strategies and customer satisfaction in e-commerce.

H2e: The involvement moderates the relationship between time risk strategies and customer satisfaction in e-commerce.

H3: The propensity to take risk moderates the relationship between legal risk reduction strategies and customer satisfaction in e-commerce during Covid-19.

H3a: The propensity to take risk moderates the relationship between perceived risk strategies and customer satisfaction in e-commerce.

H3b: The propensity to take risk moderates the relationship between price risk strategies and customer satisfaction in e-commerce.

H3c: The propensity to take risk moderates the relationship between product risk strategies and customer satisfaction in e-commerce.

H3d: The propensity to take risk moderates the relationship between legal privacy risk strategies and customer satisfaction in e-commerce.

H3e: The propensity to take risk moderates the relationship between time risk strategies and customer satisfaction in e-commerce.

Section 3: Approaches/methodology for legal risk strategies

This chapter methodology used a quantitative-based approach, and the study utilized the triangulation method for data collection. In the triangulation method, the researcher used different data sources to validate the results. Data was collected from six Gulf Cooperation Council (GCC) countries, including Bahrain, Kuwait, Oman, Qatar, Saudi Arabia, and the United Arab Emirates. In this study, the researcher utilized two methods which included primary and secondary data collection (theoretical support). The primary data consisted of a survey of online shoppers. The data collection instrument of this phase was a semi-structured script. Questionnaires were administered to a sample segment of the population of consumers who shop online from different online websites (such as Letstango.com, jadopado.com, Aido.com, etc.), in six selected countries. The question about online websites was an open-ended questionnaire. The secondary data included a literature review from the main academic research portals which included an analysis of the various theories of consumer behavior, legal acts, and models of online adoption. The research data and questionnaire were distributed among 1200 online shoppers in GCC countries, from which 1,133 internet users/online shoppers, who were classed as experienced and avid users, filled out questionnaires. In final screenings, 972 questionnaires (properly filled out) were finalized for data analysis. Their pattern of usage was as follows: 38% daily, 52% regularly, and 10% rarely. Of those surveyed, 79% have already purchased online. Based on the sample evidence, 5 out of 7 women faced a greater risk of online harassment than men. 35% of those interviewed had suffered some kind of harassment while internet chatting. For each risk criterion, women had a perception that their risk is far greater than men for all risks, except security risk, where there is no difference between the sexes. In all the risk factors considered, age was also an important distinguishing factor, at higher age, the perceived risk is stronger. In the first phase, the questionnaire tested a dozen people. This pre-test allowed us to change the wording of some questions or statements. Thereafter, two modes of distribution were made. The first researcher used pilot testing for questionnaire validation, and then distributed the questionnaire among those who responded. 972 respondents filled in the questionnaire, so the response rate was 94%. The researcher utilized two means of sources for the present research validation. The first researcher used the secondary data, in which theories and literature were used to support the results. Then the researcher utilized the survey method in which questionnaire data was collected from customers.

Section 4: Statistical analysis and results for e-commerce

4.1. Validation and robustness of regression model

The validity of this study shows that the findings truly represent the present study phenomena. The study found that the Eigen value was 0.566 i.e., less than 1. (Eigen value <1 shows that data is valid in nature). The percentage of variance should be less than 50% and the present study percentage of variance was less than 50. An F-statistic of at least 3.95 is needed to accept an alternative hypothesis. The F-statistic of the present study model was 96.23, which showed the overall significance of the regression model. The present study utilized a model of risk management strategy and its impact on customer satisfaction was, overall, significant.

4.2. Correlation analysis

Table 1: Correlation analysis of variables

Variables	M	SD	PerR	PriR	ProR	PrivR	TR	PTR	CI	CS
Perceived Risk Security	1.94	0.567	1							
Price Risk Security	2.15	0.786	0.687*	1						
Product Risk Security	1.91	0.634	0.711*	0.636*	1					
Legal Privacy Risk	2.01	0.670	0.698*	0.654*	0.759*	1				
Time Risk Security	2.19	0.946	0.493*	0.406*	0.536*	0.477*	1			
Propensity to take Risk	1.84	0.567	0.741*	0.627*	0.722*	0.556*	0.759*	1		
Customer Involvement	2.16	0.886	0.721*	0.788*	0.536*	0.453*	0.666*	0.677*	1	
Customer Satisfaction	2.11	0.544	0.546*	0.646*	0.697*	0.755*	0.456*	0.731*	0.435*	1

Description: Correlation and descriptive analysis is among the important analysis techniques used to determine the association between independent and dependent variables, and it also explains how much one variable depends on another. In the present study, correlation analysis shows that all variable correlation value lies within range (CA < 0.80) so it is stated that all variables act independently, and can be used for further analysis.

4.3. Regression Analysis

After determining the relationship between variables through correlation, regression analysis is used to assess the cause and effect relationship between dependent and independent variables. It determines how much change in a dependent variable is caused by independent variables. The regression model equations which were used by the researcher for the present study are shown below:

4.3.1. Equation for customer involvement interaction term

Customer satisfaction = $\alpha + \beta_1$ (perceived risk security) + β_2 (customer involvement) + β_3 (interaction PerR_CI) + e

Customer satisfaction = $\alpha + \beta_1$ (price risk security) + β_2 (customer involvement) + β_3 (interaction PerR_CI) + e

Customer satisfaction = $\alpha + \beta_1$ (product risk security) + β_2 (customer involvement) + β_3 (interaction ProR_CI) + e

Customer satisfaction = $\alpha + \beta_1$ (legal privacy risk) + β_2 (customer involvement) + β_3 (interaction PrivR_CI) + e

Customer satisfaction = $\alpha + \beta_1$ (time risk security) + β_2 (customer involvement) + β_3 (interaction TR_CI) + e

4.3.2. Equation for Propensity to take Risk Interaction Term

Customer satisfaction = $\alpha + \beta_1$ (perceived risk security) + β_2 (propensity to take risk) + β_3 (interaction PerR_PTR) + e

Customer satisfaction = $\alpha + \beta_1$ (price risk security) + β_2 (propensity to take risk) + β_3 (interaction PerR_PTR) + e

Customer satisfaction = $\alpha + \beta_1$ (product risk security) + β_2 (propensity to take risk) + β_3 (interaction ProR_PTR) + e

Customer satisfaction = $\alpha + \beta_1$ (legal privacy risk) + β_2 (propensity to take risk) + β_3 (interaction PrivR_PTR) + e

Customer satisfaction = $\alpha + \beta_1$ (time risk security) + β_2 (propensity to take risk) + β_3 (interaction TR_PTR) + e

In this equation, 'e' is the error term that measures the influence of variables other than independent variables.

Table 2: Regression Analysis

	Un-standardized Coefficient	Standardized Coefficient			
Variables	Beta	Beta	T	Sig	VIF
Constant	0.002		0.036	0.024	
Z score (PerR)	0.225	0.225	2.662	0.009	3.048
Z score (PriR)	0.192	0.192	2.736	0.007	2.096
Z score (ProR)	0.457	0.457	5.150	0.000	3.352
Z score (PrivR)	0.049	0.049	2.333	0.000	1.721
Z score (TR)	0.236	0.236	2.556	0.003	2.096
Z score (CI)	0.224	0.224	4.323	0.000	3.352
Z score (PTR)	0.344	0.344	0.772	0.000	1.721
Interaction PerR_CI	0.051	0.063	0.698	0.000	3.497
Interaction Pri_CI	0.080	0.087	1.109	0.000	2.593
Interaction Pro_CI	0.017	0.025	0.298	0.001	2.994
Interaction Priv_CI	0.246	0.226	5.150	0.000	2.096
Interaction TR_CI	0.254	0.244	2.333	0.003	3.352
Interaction Per_PTR	0.090	0.087	2.556	0.000	1.721
Interaction Pri_PTR	0.017	0.025	4.323	0.000	2.096
Interaction Pro_PTR	0.226	0.226	0.772	0.002	3.352
Interaction Priv_PTR	0.070	0.087	0.698	0.003	1.721
Interaction TR_PTR	0.087	0.085	1.109	0.000	3.497

Description: The study shows that the beta value of all variables shows a strong relationship between risk strategies and customer satisfaction, and also shows the moderators' impact on present relationships. The results of the present study explain that all relationships are significant in nature, as all variables (z) score P values of less than 0.05, which shows that hypotheses H1a, H1b, H1c, H1d, and H1e, are accepted, and perceived price, products, privacy and time risk securities have significant impact on customer satisfaction. Interaction terms of customer involvement and propensity to take risk are also significant, which shows that in hypotheses H2 and H3 all dimensions are accepted. Customer involvement and propensity to take risk significantly influence the relationship between risk strategies and customer satisfaction.

Table 3: Summary of Result

Hypotheses	Results	P- value	Reason of rejection
H1a: The perceived risk strategies have significant and positive impact on customer satisfaction in e-commerce	Accepted	0.009	Significant
H1b: The price risk strategies have significant and positive impact on customer satisfaction in e-commerce	Accepted	0.007	Significant
H1c: The product risk strategies have significant and positive impact on customer satisfaction in e-commerce	Accepted	0.000	Significant
H1d: The privacy risk strategies have significant and positive impact on customer satisfaction in e-commerce	Accepted	0.000	Significant
H1e: The time risk strategies have significant and positive impact on customer satisfaction in e-commerce	Accepted	0.003	Significant
H2a: The involvement moderates the relationship between perceived risk strategies and customer satisfaction in e-commerce	Accepted	0.000	Significant
H2b: The involvement moderates the relationship between price risk strategies and customer satisfaction in e-commerce	Accepted	0.000	Significant

H2c: The involvement moderates the relationship between product risk strategies and customer satisfaction in e-commerce	Accepted	0.001	Significant
H2d: The involvement moderates the relationship between privacy risk strategies and customer satisfaction in e-commerce	Accepted	0.000	Significant
H2e: The involvement moderates the relationship between time risk strategies and customer satisfaction in e-commerce	Accepted	0.003	Significant
H3a: The propensity to take risk moderates the relationship between perceived risk strategies and customer satisfaction in e-commerce	Accepted	0.000	Significant
H3b: The propensity to take risk moderates the relationship between price risk strategies and customer satisfaction in e-commerce	Accepted	0.000	Significant
H3c: The propensity to take risk moderates the relationship between product risk strategies and customer satisfaction in e-commerce	Accepted	0.002	Significant
H3d: The propensity to take risk moderates the relationship between privacy risk strategies and customer satisfaction in e-commerce	Accepted	0.003	Significant
H3e: The propensity to take risk moderates the relationship between time risk strategies and customer satisfaction in e-commerce	Accepted	0.000	Significant

Section 5: Chapter conclusions

Despite persistent cross-country differences, the Covid-19 crisis has enhanced dynamism in the e-commerce landscape across countries, and has expanded the scope of e-commerce. Theories exist to discuss the theory of perceived risk, but no theory deals with questions of change in perceived risk while using the internet. The development of assumptions of the study's questionnaire revolves around five risk dimensions in electronic commerce. These dimensions were indicative of a change in internet users' perceptions.

Thus, we realized what the characteristics of legal risk influence on customer purchase perception are. Customer satisfaction is one of the major factors studied by current research. This chapter is supported with the Global and National Commerce Act (E-SIGN Act), the Legal Action for Data Protection and Privacy Violations Act, the E-Commerce CAN-SPAM Act of 2003, and the Copyright & Trademark Act. The study represented different legal risk strategies which organizations should understand, and use to provide security to their customers, so that they get more involved with online services, and encourage the propensity to take risk, which leads towards customer satisfaction and repeat purchases. Each risk situation reveals that the cost of a book is significantly higher than buying a laptop. This would mean that if the transaction amount is higher, it is riskier for customers, and they won't want to share their credit card numbers and their personal information online. This is because of risks which customers perceive during their online transactions. Indeed, in 2004, risks related to learning (lost time) and consumption patterns (product risk and intimacy) are based on customer satisfaction. If a customer is satisfied with his internet transactions, he becomes a risk taker. This chapter examined the impact of legal risk-taking strategies which involve perceived, product, price, legal privacy and time risk security, and investigated these strategies' influence on customer satisfaction. The study explained that these strategies (confidentiality, time security, no visual distortion of product) taken by organizations have a major influence on customer satisfaction, and this relationship is influenced by customer involvement and their variable propensity to take risk. Data was collected from internet users/online shoppers from GCC countries during Covid-19. 972 respondents filled out the questionnaire, so the response rate was 94%. The researcher utilized two sources for research validation. First, the researcher used secondary data in which theories and literature were used to support the results, then a survey method in which questionnaire data was collected from customers. Many sites provide clear information on safety, but more than half do not provide this information clearly and in a way that is sufficiently accessible. It is therefore imperative for merchants and retailers to review the usability of their websites, and put forward safety tools that are visible to all users, such as signs, labels, and certifications. It is important for organizations to build their security systems and provide a good customer experience and a less risky online environment, so that the more customers get involved with the product, the more they will be satisfied, and repurchase, which is an important tactic to be used during Covid-19. Future study should include more risk dimensions and should also increase the study sample, which would be helpful to increase the generalizability of the study.

The practical implications of the chapter:

According to critical analysis of the topic and results, legal risk is very important in GCC countries which ultimately influence the customer involvement, satisfaction and purchasing behavior. GCC countries should attempt to create a coherent legal and regulatory framework (lessons can be learnt from the EU). This will help to reduce the legal risk and remove the obstacles to the growth of e-commerce in GCC countries, affirming a certain level of transparency by imposing prior information requirements for electronic contracts, as well as regulating commercial communication and advertisements and regulating consumers' technical errors. This system will also help to regulate the liabilities of intermediary service providers, as well as the right of withdrawal rules. Furthermore, GCC countries should create an efficient system of ODR that will help to build trust in online transactions and preserve online business relationships in the long term.

References

Ariff M.S.M, Sylvester M, Zakuan N, Ismail K And Ali, K.M, (2014), Consumer Perceived Risk, Attitude And Online Shopping Behavior; Empirical Evidence From Malaysia, IOP Conference Series: Materials Science And Engineering

Barr, David D. (2000), "The Need of a Broad Standard in Global E-Commerce" The Internet Law Journal, Dec. 26,

Bateson John E. G. And Hoffman, K. Douglas. (2001) Marketing Service: Bookman.

Bianchi & Mathews. (2016). Internet Marketing And Export Market Growth In Chile. *Journal Of Business Research* **69**, 426-434.

Bond, Robert, "International Legal Issues of E-Commerce" Legal Updates, http://www.faegre.com, 2003.

Choi, H., Kim, Y. And Kim, J. (2011), "Driving Factors Of Post Adoption Behavior In Mobile Data Services", Journal Of Business Research, Vol. 64 No. 11, Pp. 1212-7.

Cunningham, L.F., Gerlach, J.H., Harper, M.D., Young, C.E. (2005), "Perceived Risk And The Consumer Buying Process: Internet Airline Reservations", International Journal Of Service Industry Management, Vol. 16 No.4, Pp.357-72.

Dholakia, Utpal M. (1997) An Investigation Of The Relationship Between Perceived Risk And Product Involvement. Advances In Consumer Research, V. 24, P.159-167.

Engel, James F.; Blackwell, Roger D. And Miniard, Paul W. (1995) Consumer Behavior. 8. Ed. Orlando: The Dryden Press. 951 P. Bibliography: P. 441 - 442.

Gierl, H., Hammer, C. (2003), "Fear Of Loss Of Anonymity On The Internet And Consumers' Reactions: An Empirical Investigation", Yearbook Of Marketing And Consumer Research, Vol. 1 Pp.89-106.

Kim, E., Hong, T., (2010). Segmenting Customers In Online Stores From Factors That Affect The Customer's Intention To Purchase., Pp. 383-388

Kim, L.H., Kim, D.J., Leong, J.K. (2005), "The Effect Of Perceived Risk On Purchase Intention In Purchasing Airline Tickets Online", Journal Of Hospitality & Leisure Marketing, Vol. 13 No.2, Pp.33-53.

Klein, H. E Sterk, E.C. (2003) "At Risk" Women Who Think That They Have No Chance Of Getting HIV: Self-Assessed Perceived Risks. Woman And Health, V.38, N.2, P.47-63

Kovacs .M, Farias .H. (2002). Perceived Risks And Ways To Purchase: The Duality Versus Internet Consumers Online. Journal Of Economics And Management, V.1, N.2, April / June

Kuo Y F, Hu T L., & Yang, S. C. (2013) Effects Of Inertia And Satisfaction In Female Online Shoppers On Repeat-Purchase Intention. Managing Service Quality: An International Journal.168 – 187

Laroche, M., Bergeron, J. And Goutaland, C. (2004) How Intangibility Affects Perceived Risk: The Moderating Role Of Knowledge And Involvement. The Journal Of Services Marketing, V.17, N.2 / 3, P.122-141.

Lim, N. (2003), "Consumer Perceived Risk: Sources Versus Consequences", Electronic Consumer Research And Applications, Vol. 2 Pp.216-28.

Lim, Y. J, Osman, A, Salahuddin, S.N, Romle A. R, Abdullah. S, (2016), Factors Influencing Online Shopping Behavior: The Mediating Role Of Purchase Intention, Procedia Economics And Finance, Vol 32, 401- 410

Mccole, P., Ramsey, E. And Williams, J. (2010), "Trust Considerations On Attitudes Towards Online Purchasing: The Moderating Effect Of Privacy And Security Concerns", Journal Of Business Research, Vol. 63 Nos 9/10, Pp. 1018-24.

Mercado & Rajagopal. (2015). Driving Consumers Toward Online Retailing Technology: Analyzing Myths And Realities. *Journal Of Transnational Management* **20**, 155-171.

Mitchell, V.-W. (1998) A Role For Consumer Risk Perceptions In Grocery Retailing. British Food Journal, N.4, P.171-183.

Mitchell, V.-W. And Greatorex, M. (1990) Consumer Purchasing In Foreign Countries: The Perceived Risk Perspective. International Journal Of Advertising, V.9, N.4, P.295-307.

Mou, Shin & Cohen. (2015). Trust And Risk In Consumer Acceptance Of E-Services. *Electronic Commerce Research* .

Nasir, M. A, (2004), LEGAL ISSUES INVOLVED IN E-COMMERCE, Journal of Ubiquity, Volume 4, Issue 49

Oliver, Richard L. Satisfaction: (1997) A Behavioral Perspective On The Consumer. New York: McGraw-Hill Company.

Park, I., Bhatnagar, A. And Rao, H.R. (2010), "Assurance Seals, On-Line Customer Satisfaction, And Repurchase Intention", International Journal Of Electronic Commerce, Vol. 14 No. 3, Pp. 11-34.

Peter, S and Deveaux, S, (2000), "Jurisdiction in Cyberspace" IDG News Service, see also http://www.pcwo

Ranaweera. (2016). Perspective Of Trust Towards E-Government Initiatives In Sri Lanka. *Springerplus* **5**. .

Robert, C and Thomas, U, (2000), Law & Economics, 3rd edition, Addison Wesley, pp. 336.

Santos, J. (2002), "From Intangibility To Tangibility On Service Quality Perceptions: A Comparison Study Between Consumers And Service Providers In Four Service Industries", Managing Service Quality, Vol. 12 No.5, Pp.292-302.

Schiffman J.B And Kanuk. L. L (1997) Consumer Behavior Published By Prentice Hall Sixth Edition .446

Singh, A. (2018). E-Commerce interfering with Privacy: Perceived Risks and Security issues with Techno-policy outcomes. In Digital Transformation Strategies and trends in E-learning: Privacy, Preservation and Policy (1st ed., pp. 802-823).

Sobihah M, Mohamad M, Ali N. A. M, Ismail W. Z. W (2015), E-Commerce Service Quality On Customer Satisfaction, Belief And Loyalty: A Proposal, *Mediterranean Journal Of Social Sciences,* Vol 2

Solomon (2002) The Consumer Behavior: Buying, Having Being. 5 Ed. Porto Alegre: Bookman, P.446. Bibliography: P.216-217

Solomon, Michael R. (1998) Consumer Behavior: Buying, Having And Being. 4. Ed. New Jersey: Prentice Hall. 640 P: P.280-281

Son, M. And Han, K. (2011), "Beyond The Technology Adoption: Technology Readiness Effects On Post-Adoption Behavior", Journal Of Business Research, Vol. 64 No. 11, Pp. 1178-82.

Wu, George, Jiao. Z, And Richard. G, (2004), "Decision Under Risk," In Blackwell Handbook Of Judgment And Decision Making, Nigel Harvey And Derek Koehler, Eds. London: Blackwell Publishing, Forthcoming.

Zeithaml, V.A., Bitner, M.J. (2003), Services Marketing: Integrating Customer Focus Across The Firm, 3rd Ed., McGraw-Hill, New York, NY.

Appendix (A)

- ✓ Bahrain Legislative Decree No.28 of 2002 with respect to Electronic Transactions
- ✓ Dubai Electronic Transactions and Commerce Law (2002)
- ✓ Kuwaiti electronic transaction law no 20/2014
- ✓ Oman's Electronic Transactions Law, Royal Decree 69/2008
- ✓ Qatar Decree Law No. 16 of 2010 on the Promulgation of the Electronic Commerce and Transactions Law
- ✓ Rules of the Bahrain Trade Act (7/1987) (GCC Legal Information Network 2011)
- ✓ Saudi Arbitration Law Royal Decree No M/34, April 2012
- ✓ Saudi Electronic Transactions Law, Royal Decree No. M/8 (26 March 2007)
- ✓ Saudi Implementation Regulations for the Electronic Transaction Law (2007) MCIT Resolution No. 2 2008
- ✓ United Arab Emirates Electronic Commerce and Transactions Law (2006) Federal Law No. (1)

CHAPTER 2

FEAR AND UNCERTAINTY EFFECTS OF THE COVID-19 CRISIS

Summary of Chapter Two

This chapter explains the effect of the coronavirus crisis (US Covid-19), the fear index, and oil price, on the United States equity market price. The study first used the novel proxy of the fear index (Infectious Disease EMV index) developed by Baker et al. (2020). Data from 21 January 2020, which was the start of the new coronavirus (Covid-19) in America (US), up until 6 July 2020, was collected. The study used the Nonlinear Autoregressive distributed lag model (NARDL) to confirm the causal factors (short-long run) of DJI. The result depicts that two out three exogenous (independent) variables (US Covid-19 and Infectious Disease EMV) significantly related negatively to being co-integrated with the United States equity market (DJI) in both positive and negative shocks, whereas IDEMV negative shock was insignificant. Oil was significantly positively co-integrated with the DJI index in both positive and negative. In the case of long term co-integration, all variables - oil, US Covid-19, and Infectious Disease EMV are significantly co-integrated in the case of positive shocks, but insignificantly in case of negative shocks. This study is beneficial for individual and government investors by identifying an important investment (the Infectious Disease EMV index) when they want to diversify their portfolio.

Keywords: fear index, IDEMV, oil price, coronavirus (US Covid-19)

Section 1: Introduction

After internationalization, all financial markets are co-integrated, contagious, and more vulnerable to different external and internal events like disasters, news, environmental, and sports and political events (Godil, Sarwat, Sharif, & Jermsittiparsert 2020, Andrei & Hasler 2015, Zheng 2014). The entire world equity market suffered during the period of the natural disaster called coronavirus (nCovid-19), which depicted a mountain outsell-off bind to

Covid-19. The FSTE 100 and DJIA index saw the biggest drops since 1987 (25 percent and 25 percent, respectively) (Barro, Ursúa, & Weng 2020). The epidemic Covid-19 respiratory disease (SARS-CoV-2) started in China. It affected human health, and also exponentially increased economic costs. The numbers of infected people and deaths around the world are currently 45,566,956 and 304,201 respectively. The most common symptoms of the nCovid-19 virus infection include coughing, shortness of breath, and high fever, and the average duration of the virus in the human body remains between 1 and 14 days (Meninno & Wolff 2020). According to the WHO's latest update, nCovid-19 is unstoppable, and new viruses will never end. The WHO declared an emergency and mandated vaccinations to cure people infected with Covid-19. Beyond the severe impact on human health, this new epidemic hinders the social-economic welfare and economic performance of countries. According to a research study conducted by the National Academy of Sciences (US), the overall income loss around the world due to Covid-19 exceeds 60 billion dollars (Nishiura at el. 2020). A report issued by the World Bank, divides the loss due to Covid-19 into four major categories: 1) reduction of the labor force and increased deaths; 2) labor production decreased sharply; 3) resource requirements for Covid-19 control and cure; and 4) the heavy amount of loss borne by individuals due to prevention policy and closure of production units. Covid-19 not only affects developing countries; the United States and Europe are the most infected countries (Godil et al. 2020). Climate change and weather conditions across the US and Europe may further contribute to the spread of Covid-19 (Epstein 2001). Among the infected countries, America is the top of the list with the highest number of people (468,895), and the numbers have grown exponentially. The US alone accounts for almost 33% of the total infected people in the entire world (Alqahtani & Martinez 2020). The Covid-19 news badly affected the united stock market; the DJIA index lost 35% of its value within a month (Barro, Ursúa, & Weng 2020).

Figure 1: Daily DJI index closing prices from 22-01-2020 to 14-05-2020

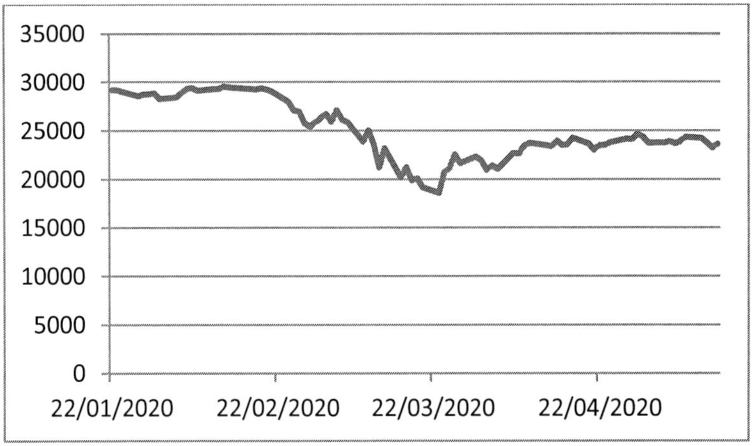

News-based events shape equity market performance. The EMH hypothesis pointed out that a spread of an equal amount of news to all market participants, but an unequal distribution of news, creates uncertainty for equity market performance. According to Li (2018), news-based uncertainty could affect investors' consumption and portfolio decisions, which leads to a change in asset prices. Moreover, investors are more conscious of negative news, as compared to positive news. Therefore, accurately predicting the behavior of news-based economic market volatility and its causal relationship with the financial market is the major task for risk managers, financial economics professionals, and researchers. Due to the great destruction in the economy by coronavirus, a new type of news-based index has been created, called the Infectious Disease EMV index (Baker et al. 2020), which shows the news EMV related to natural disasters, including flu viruses, and epidemics such as coronavirus, MERS, Ebola, SARS, H5N1, and H1N1. In a recent paper, we tried to answer an important question of how commodities (such as oil), the fear indexes (EMV and the Infectious Disease EMV index) and coronavirus news, asymmetrically impact the equity market of the United States.

The American equity market index DJIA reached 30,000 points during February 2020, which was its highest level for the last 100 years. When the equity market leptokurtic (positive returns) trends, individuals are optimistic and business performance further increases. On the other hand, when the equity market shows platykurtic (negative returns), volatility is enhanced. This is also known as the leverage effect. When negative news related to negative returns is spread in the market, investors show herd mentality and reluctance to invest in any market. Due to the importance of news in the international equity market, a new type of index was created, known as the Equity Market Volatility (EMV) index, which was created by Baker, Bloom, Davis, and Kost (2019). Scant academic studies to examine the type of association between EMV and equity market of countries are still available (Meninno & Wolff 2020, Zhu, Liu, Wang, Wei, & Wei 2019). Alqahtani, Wither, Dong, and Goodwin (2020) pointed out that no co-integration prevails between the equity market and EMV. No evidence of a clear association between EMV and equity market is found in the literature. A new type of fear index was created in March 2020, known as the Infectious Disease Equity Market Volatility (EMV) index, created by Baker et al. (2020) based on the concept of EMV. This index is the extension of the first EMV index, and incorporates the news related to infectious disease. The new index tells us how much equity market volatility is created due to natural disasters or different infectious diseases. There is no current study of this index, so ours is the very first, innovative work which uses the Infectious Disease Equity Market Volatility (EMV) index and checks its association with the United States equity market.

Infectious diseases are directly associated with the equity market because these disasters can close production units due to the large numbers of deaths. During the Covid-19 epidemic, economic growth was affected and oil prices are now higher than ever in history. Oil is the main ingredient of all production units. When there is a change in oil prices, the whole economy of any country may be affected, directly or indirectly, and literature proves this.

During the coronavirus period, the entire world's economies suffered because the change in oil prices increased uncertainty (volatility), and hindered equity market performance. So, in our recent study, we are going to examine the effect of coronavirus news, the fear index, and oil prices on the United States equity market's performance by employing the nonlinear autoregressive distributed lag (NARDL) model introduced by Shin et al. (2014). Our study makes several contributions to the finance literature. Death and case rates were soaring day-by-day, especially in the United States. Investors' sentiment was badly affected during Covid-19, and the performance of financial markets around the globe was inversely affected. Financial product prices showed a downward trend. Black wrote about these negative returns (1976), in a study in which he pointed out that equity return was negatively associated with financial asset's volatility, which is also called the leverage effect. Most assets show negative prices during the period of negative, as compared to positive, news. Most recent studies ignore the Covid-19 news factor and ignore the role of investors' sentiment on equity market performance. Investors behave irrationally during any pandemic, and the stock market is directly affected. So, the first contribution of the study was to use coronavirus (Covid-19) news data to investigate the role of the news on stock market prices. Secondly, our study used the EMV index which is very rarely used in literature, because it was only developed in 2019 and the findings are not clear. Thirdly, the most important contribution is that our study incorporated the Infectious Disease Equity Market Volatility (EMV) index, which was created in March 2020, and no study had used this index before. Fourthly, the present study selected the United States stock market, because the US is the economic power of the world. The source of the 2007/8 financial crisis was the US financial market, so any change in the equity market performance of the United States could affect the entire world. So, our study was new by incorporating this index and tried to examine this index relationship with the United States equity market. The last contribution was methodological as we used a nonlinear autoregressive distributed lag (NARDL) model based upon a co-integrated time series in our paper. This method is better, compared to the autoregressive distributed lag (ARDL) model, because the ARDL targets linearity problem. In reality, mostly finance data is non-linear and normal as well. So, the NARDL model is used to capture the asymmetric (non-linear) relationship between the variables of the study, and the model also captures the long and short-run asymmetries. Importantly, our model does not suffer the problem of standard bond testing procedure (Fetzer, Hensel, Hermle & Roth 2020, Andrei, & Hasler 2015, Bloom 2009) to question long term effects between target variables regardless of the integration order of the variables concerned. Due to these advantages, our study decided to use NARDL to decide the asymmetric relationship between United States coronavirus news, IDEMV, oil prices, and the United States equity market (DJI index).

The remaining part of the study is arranged as follows: Section two discusses the literature review, and Section three provides information about methodology and data. Section four reports discussion of the results and findings, while Section five concludes.

Section 2: The Coronavirus Crisis, the Fear Index, and Oil Price Theories

News plays an important role in the equity market because investors' behavior totally changed during the negative and positive information spillover. In other words, investors' behavior is highly dependent on the news. First, an initial study conducted by Niederh (1971) concluded that news greatly and significantly influences the performance of the stock market and investors' investment decisions. Black (1976) pointed out that a negative association exists between equity market prices and their volatility; the term known as leverage theory. Some researchers conclude that volatility is increased by forthcoming negative news (Hung 2019, Zhu, Liu, et al. 2019, Badeeb & Lean 2018, Smales 2017), while other studies contradict the relationship between volatility and investors' fear through news, so conclude there is no relationship between investors' fear and equity prices. Epstein (2001) pointed out that investors' distress creates more volatility in the financial market by showing panic behavior. Zheng (2014) revealed that significant and negative relationships were found between investors' sentiments and equity market performance. This study used the VIX index prices to measure an investor's sentiments. Another study result is contradictory, and pointed to a significant, positive relationship between market volatility (the VIX index as representative of the fear index) and the returns of the equity market (Fleming et al. 1995). Smales' study (2017) tried to investigate investors' fear (sentiments) and equity market price by using the ARDL model. According to Li (2018), the news from governmental media has a higher intensity impact than other media, which raises a concern that positive news enhances the returns of the equity market, and vice versa. The result is also consistent with a paper (Su, Fang, Yin, 2018) which concluded that new-based volatility (NVIX) creates much higher volatility in the equity market, compared to financial uncertainty (FU). Cepoi (2020) developed a special fear index due to Covid-19 and also investigated the impact on the equity market price pattern. Mejova, & Kalimeri (2020) studied the impact of word-of-mouth on investors' behavior. Data was collected from Facebook, and concluded that a spread of misinformation inversely impacts business and individual behavior. Their study developed an index of special fear due to Covid-19 and also investigated the impact on the equity market price pattern. The study used panel data and conclusion to confirm the significant role in determining the market price of the stock market. Zhu et al. (2019) recently conducted a study to clear the picture between stock market return and fear index. Two proxies were used (VIX and EMV) and results revealed the fact that EMV creates very low volatility (minimal) which should be ignored. The literature studies result is matched with the arguments of Pal and Mitra (2015), who pointed out that the return of the equity market and volatility could be anything (negative or positive) over a specific period.

There is scant literature investigating the relationship between oil, coronavirus, natural disaster, and the equity market (Barro, Ursúa & Weng 2020, Zhu, Liu, Wang, Wei, & Wei 2019, Baker, Bloom, & Davis 2016, Solomon 2012). Oil and volatility in the global market remain a serious concern for economists (Kumar 2019, Fang, Qian, Chen & Yu 2018, Andrei, & Hasler 2015). A study by Pal and Mitra (2015) pointed out that those infectious diseases (SARS, HINI, and dengue fever) have not only the ability to affect human health, but inversely affect the country's economic growth. The study results also indicate that investor rationale (behavior) deviates during the outbreak of different infectious diseases. The basic rationale for equity prices, suggests that the price of oil will automatically affect the cash flow of individual companies, and hence cause a change in their stock prices (Jones & Kaul 1996). Bloom (2009) conducted their research study to determine the type of association between equity price volatility and the outbreak of different natural disasters by using the GARCH methodology. The data for the study was collected from Australia from 1980 to 2003. The conclusion supports the idea that natural disaster outbreaks in a country bring volatility in equity prices. Hamdan and Hamdan (2018) conducted their study in Saudi Arabia, and the major purpose of the paper was to investigate the major ingredients (causes) that create volatility in the equity market. The research paper used data specific to the period 2007 to 2016, and employed the causality test. The study found that oil causes significant volatility in the Saudi Arabian equity market. While Yin and Feng's (2019) finding reveals that no predictive association exists between the volatility of the stock market and the price of oil, Hoque et al. (2019) suggest that a significant association exists between oil price and investors' uncertainty (EPU) in the case of Malaysian equity market prices. Two studies, by Conlon and McGee (2020) and Gharib, Mefteh-Wali, and Jabeur (2020), conducted cross correlation between the equity market and oil, before and after Covid-19, and found no correlation existed during Covid-19. Barro et al. (2020) conducted their study in order to investigate the psychological effect of the spread of Covid-19. The study results showed that investors behave differently during a pandemic. The intensity of fear suddenly increased during Covid-19. A recent study conducted by Al-Awadhi et al. (2020) proved that Covid-19 created massive volatility in China's equity market. Another recent study by Fetzer et al. (2020) tried to investigate the relationship between the infectious disease EMV index and electricity volatility. The study used the recent data from 3 March to 6 April 2020. The results indicated that the energy market is highly influenced by the volatility in the infectious disease EMV index.

Based on the previous literature review, the relationship between investors' fear, oil prices, natural disasters, and equity market volatility was found to be inconclusive. Very few studies used these variables in their studies. Moreover, our study is the first using the infectious disease EMV index together with other EMV indices during the current pandemic environment. So, this first innovative study used the fear index (EMV index and their sub-indices including the infectious disease EMV index), oil prices, and coronavirus, and checked their impact on the equity market of the super country (United States).

Literature review summary Table 2.1

Research Studies	**Sample Countries**	**Data**	**Aims/ Objective**	**Key conclusions**
Al-Awadhi, Al-Saifi, Al-Awadhi, &Alhamadi, (2020)	China	10 Jan – 31 Jan 2020	The current research paper tries to examine spillover and the contagious relationship between the equity market and Covid-19 by using panel regression.	The results depict that the death ratio and infected cases have a negative significant relationship with China's equity market performance.
Nikkinen, & Peltomäki (2020)	United States	Jan, 2016 (weekly data)	In the current study, the author wanted to explore the information (demand and supply factor) and crash fear.	The finding told that individual web search is directly linked with the equity market and VIX.
Alqahtani, Wither, Dong, & Goodwin, (2020)	India, Hong Kong, and China	2001 – 2018	The main objective of this paper is to search out the nature of asymmetric correlation (co-integration) between international equity (three countries) market and a news based (fear) index by using the model of NARDL.	The conclusion of the paper reveals that negative non-linear relationship between the variables of this study except for the country of China.
Fetzer, Hensel, Hermle, & Roth (2020)	Worldwide (global) dataset	Feb 19, 2020 – March 16, 2020	The study's major and core objective to analyze the stress factor related to economic activity and Covid-19.	The research study result pointed out that stress factors related to economic activity exponentially increased by increasing Covid-19. Economic stress could be reduced by educating and giving awareness related to Covid-19.

Mo, Mu, & Zhang (2019)	China	2005 – 2017	The current academic study explores the correlation between macroeconomic ingredients, prices of oil, and equity market.	Research reveals that 3 macroeconomic ingredients, the exchange rate is the first in the ranking of a significant relationship with the China equity market during the bearish (stormy) period.
Zhu, Liu, Wang, Wei, & Wei (2019)	The United States four stock markets	1990 – 2019	This paper analyzed the type of spillover relationship between VIX, EMV, and equity market of the US by employing GARCH-MIDAS.	The fear index study results show that the VIX index has comparatively great magnitude effects on the US equity market than the EMV index.
Mo, Mu & Zhang (2019)	United States	1980 – 2016	The research investigates the nature of volatility related to implied new based volatility and equity market of the US.	The conclusion statements state that weak short term volatility presents while strong volatility exists between implied new based volatility and equity market of the US.
Fang, Qian, Chen & Yu (2018)	France, Italy, US, Japan, UK, Canada, and Germany	1998 – 2016	The research paper's major aim to investigate the response by NVIX in the equity market.	The academic paper concludes that only long term and significant associations present between NVIX and equity market.
Li (2018)	China	Feb, 2017-April 2017 (intraday data)	The current research article core and the main purpose is to examine the relationship between the China equity market and news by employing OLS.	The result confirms the fact that positive endorse performance of China's equity while positive has an inverse impact on the equity market.

Smales (2017)	USA	Jan1990-Dec2015	The present research paper tried to guess the importance of investors' fear (sentiments) and equity market by using the ARDL model.	The finding reveals that short-run investors panic when any negative news comes compared to the long term.
Andrei &Hasler (2015)	Theoretical paper	1969-2012	The present theoretical paper examines explore equity market volatility and investors' attraction.	If returns variance of equity market exponentially increase investor panic behavior and uncertainty enhanced.
Pal & Mitra (2015)	US	1990 - 2012	The current paper has tried to examine the co-integration between the WTI oil market and the equity market of the US.	Oil is the main (key) input of every sector, therefore result indicates and gives the direction of the presence of co-integration between concerned variables of the study.
Peress (2014)	OECD Countries	1989 - 2010	The author tried to investigate the nature of the relationship (causal effects) between information from different media and equity markets.	The results depict that information helps to increase the efficiency of different markets, so highly suggested to improve the source of provided media information.
Solomon (2012)	IR firms	2002 - 2007	The present academic paper wanted to examine the core relationship behavior between equity price and publicity selectivity (bad and good media coverage).	The conclusion consistent and prove the causal effect of IR firms on media return and their coverage as well.

Chen, Chen, Tang, & Huang (2009)	Taiwan	Sep 2002 – May 2003	The present research wanted to inquire about the negative and positive impact of SARS on the equity market.	The conclusion reveals that the SARS turmoil period spread negatively related to some sectors which include retail and wholesale sectors. While positive shock has observed in the biotechnology sector.
Sadorsky (1999)	U.S	1947 – 1996	One of the initial study which aimed to examine between equity and oil market.	OV and OP have a strong relationship with the equity market.

Section 3: Methodological Contribution

This study examines the asymmetric (non-linear) long and short rum impact of United States Covid-19 news, IDEMV, and oil prices on the United States equity market (DJI index). The basic equation is given below:

$$\mathrm{DJI} = \mathrm{f}(USCOVID - 19^{+}, USCOVID - 19^{-}, OIL^{+}, OIL^{-}, IDEMV^{+}, IDEMV^{-})$$

The non-linear ARDL (NARDL) model is presented by Shin et al. (2014) and employed to test the long and short-run dynamic relationship between variables of interest. Our model is robust in the scene, can be applied to a smaller sample size, and the order of integration cannot matter. The unit root test is used to verify the order of integration in our particular study. More importantly, positive and negative elements cover asymmetric, and additionally, also cover extreme events like the financial crisis period, etc. (Raza, Shahzad, Tiwari, & Shahbaz 2016). The simple equation given by Shin et al. (2014) is:

$$\mathrm{Y_t} = (x_0 + \gamma x_t^{+} + \gamma x_t^{-} + u_t)(3.1)$$

Where $\gamma^{+}$and $\gamma^{-}$are considered long-term parameters of kx1 vector of independent variables (regressors) *xt*, which are decomposed as:

$$\mathrm{X_t} = (x_0 + x_t^{+} + x_t^{-}) \qquad (3.2)$$

Where + *xt*,(−*xt*) are the partial sums of positive (negative) change in *xt*as follows:

$$X_t^{+} = \sum_{i=1}^{t} \Delta x_i^{+} = \sum_{i=1}^{t} \max\,(\Delta x_{i,0)}\ (3.3)$$

$$X_t^{-} = \sum_{i=1}^{t} \Delta x_i^{-} = \sum_{i=1}^{t} \min(\Delta x_{i,0)}$$

The NARDL (V,W) Equation (3.4) form, the present form of non-linear (asymmetric) error correction model (AECM) can be categorized as

$$\Delta Y_t = vY_{t-1} + \sigma^{+} x_{t-1}^{-} + \sum_{i=1}^{v-1} \tau j \Delta y_{i-1} + \sum_{i=0}^{w} (\pi_i^{+} \Delta x_{t-l}^{+} + \pi_i^{-} \Delta x_{t-l}^{-}) + u_t(3.4)$$

Where $\sigma^{+} = -v\,\gamma^{+}$ *and* $\sigma^{-} = -v\,\gamma^{-}$

Finally, the asymmetric (non-linear) aggregate dynamic and the multiplier effect of a specific unit change in $x_t{}^{+}andx_t{}^{-}t$ and – *yt* can be examined respectively, using the way given below:

$$n_h{}^{+} = \sum_{i=1}^{h} \frac{\delta yt+i}{\delta xt+}, n_h{}^{-} = \sum_{i=1}^{h} \frac{\delta yt+i}{\delta xt-}, \text{h}= 0, 1, 2\ldots..$$

Section 4: Graphical Representation of Data

The study decided to use the daily value of all variables including the Dow Jones index of the United States, daily searches of Google for coronavirus news in the United States (US Covid-19), oil prices, the Economic Market Volatility (EMV) index, and daily data from one sub-indices infectious disease index. The data is collected from 22 January to 6 July 2020, and all data is collected from Yahoo finance and Fred websites. The EMV index is a new and recently developed index based on the text of a United States paper given by Baker et al. in 2019 to measure volatility in the equity market of the US. Thirty-one sub-indexes, and their related news affecting the financial market volatility, were also added into the EMV index. Recently, an update was made to the EMV index, due to the outbreak of the new coronavirus, and the infectious disease index was added as a sub-index in the overall EMV presented by Baker et al. in 2020. By adding the infectious disease index into the EMV indices, pandemics, SARS, Ebola, MERS, Covid-19 (and five other types), H1N1, H5N1, and flu news are also added, and this news created volatility in the US equity market.

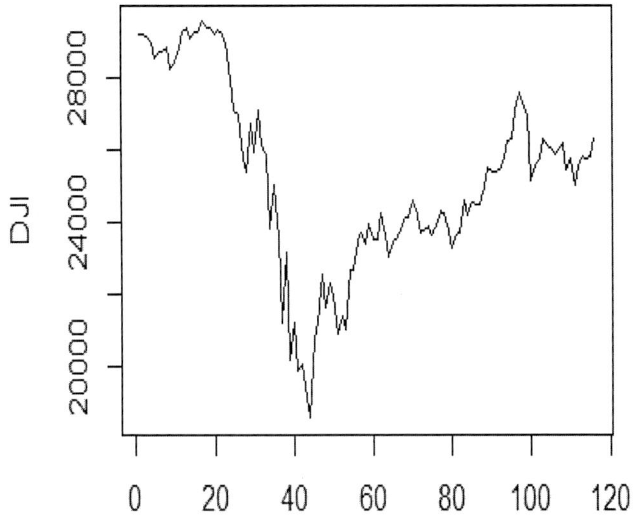
DJI
20000
24000
28000
0
20
40
60
80
100
120

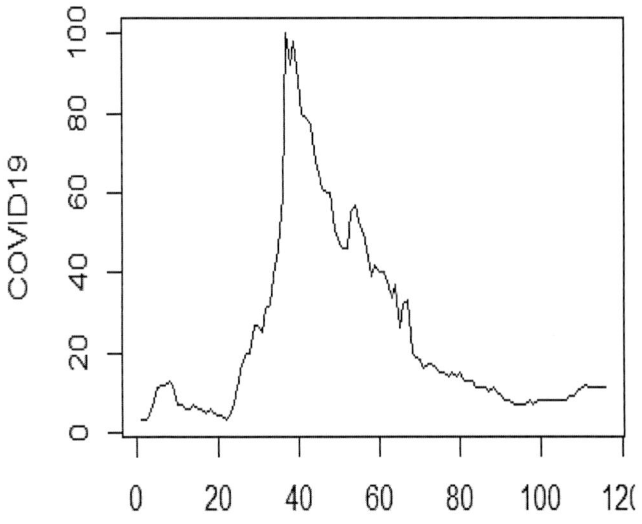
COVID19
0
20
40
60
80
100
0
20
40
60
80
100
12(

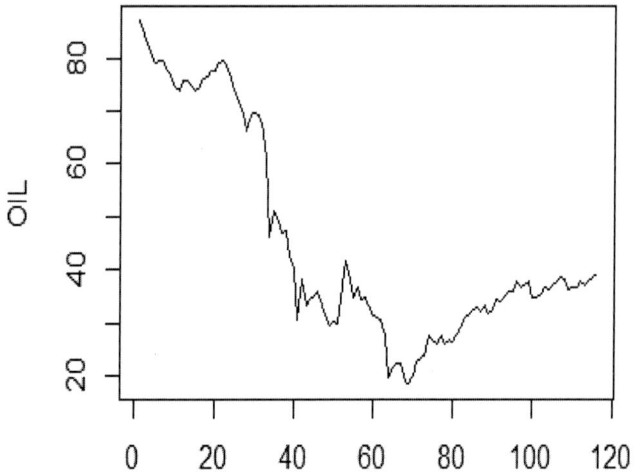

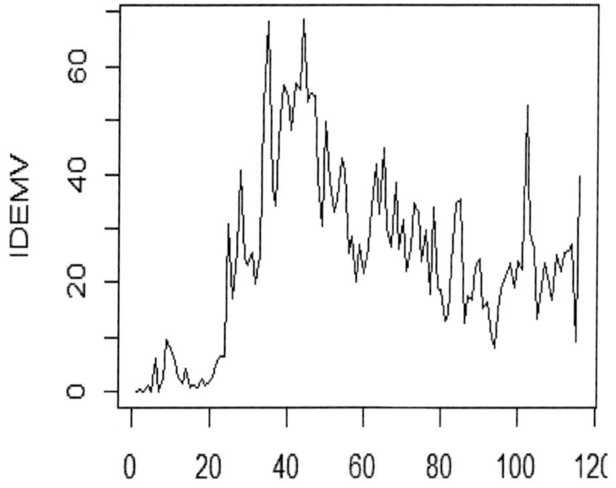

All variables individual time series graphs are shown during the Covid-19 period (22 Jan - 20 May). It has been observed that all variables show a huge variation, and show non-linear. Some variables have an upward trend, while others showed a downward trend, which confirms the asymmetric behavior of data.

Section 5: Analysis, Discussion and Results

This part contains results and discussion, a descriptive statistic correlation matrix and the NARDL model and other tests used in this study.

Table 4.1: Descriptive statistics summary

	DJI	USCOVID_19	OIL	IDEMV
Mean	25095.86	381929.1	33.36835	26.16565
Median	24256.45	14250.00	28.70000	26.38000
Maximum	29440.47	1528568.	58.34000	68.37000
Minimum	19028.36	1.000000	-37.63	0.000000
Std. Dev.	3114.344	515216.2	16.21736	18.48145
Skewness	0.108179	0.975371	-0.73449	0.211439
Kurtosis	1.793385	2.388423	5.362189	2.169537

The descriptive statistics result shows that the US Covid-19 and DJI index has the highest mean values (381929.1, 25095.86) and greater dispersion, 515216.2 and 3114.344 respectively, which shows that both of these variables are quite dispersed and far away from their average values. Moreover, the oil price values deviate from the bell shape and show highly negative skewed and leptokurtic behavior, which shows that oil prices went down during the coronavirus period.

Table 4.2 contains the results of two Narayan and Popp (2010) structural break unit root tests, to gain information regarding the stationary point of the variables used in our paper. While using conventional unit root tests, the value of R square is too high (spurious regression). In order to avoid this problem, our study used endogenously determined structural break Narayan and Popp tests (2010). The results of model 1 (break in intercept) and model 2 (break in intercept and trend) depict that there is no variable stationary point at level, the whole of the variables (DJI, US Covid-19, IDEMV, and OIL) are stationary at first difference. All the structural breaks of DJI and OIL (M1 and M2) are in the month of March, which depicts that oil prices fell due to large oil supply and shortage of demand, due to the outbreak of

Covid-19. The DJI breaks in March show that, due to Covid-19, all production units stopped, which lowered the performance of DJI by up to 35 percent during March. Covid-19 structural breaks and the number of cases both peak during the month of May. So, this means we can use the NARDL model to check the impact of all independent variables on the DJI index. But before that, we need to apply the bound test to know about the presence of co-integration. Table 4.3 confirms the presence of co-integration in our dependent variable, so we can surely apply the NARDL model in this paper.

Table 4.2: Narayan and Popp (2010) results at the intercept, intercept and trend

Variables	Break in intercept				Break in intercept and trend			
	t-statistic	TB1	TB2	K	t-statistic	TB1	TB2	K
DJI	-3.816	5/03/2020	23/03/2020	0	-5.961	16/03/2020	21/03/2020	0
USCOVID_19	−12.520	30/04/2020	2/05/2020	5	−7.003	6/05/2020	15/05/2020	2
OIL	−2.169	11/03/2020	29/03/2020	3	−3.559	31/03/2020	12/04/2020	1
IDEMV	−6.304	28/04/2020	18/05/2020	0	−5.249	1/05/2020	28/05/2020	0

Notes: ***, ** indicate the p-value 1% and 5% null hypothesis criteria for unit root

Table 4.3: bound (co-integration) test

Exploratory variable	F-statistics value	K	Lower-Bound value (90%)	Upper-Bound value (90%)	End conclusion
Dow Jones index (DJI)	6.192585	3	3.77	5.61	Presence of Cointegration

Table 4.4: NARDL model results

	short run asymmetry				Long run asymmetry			
Variable	Coefficient	Std. Error	t-Statistic	Prob.	Coefficient	Std. Error	t-Statistic	Prob.
$IDEMV^{+}$	-23.40671	7.015391	-3.33649	0.0013**	-129.09060	30.56938	-4.2228	0.0001*
$IDEMV^{-}$	2.08718	7.91494	0.26370	0.79250	-6.14379	22.91100	-0.26816	0.78910
$COV19^{+}$	-56.63202	16.49060	-3.43420	0.00090*	-75.67362	26.36366	-2.87038	0.00500*
$COV19^{-}$	-74.68131	28.86760	-2.58703	0.01110**	-28.61110	33.65200	-0.85021	0.39720
OIL^{+}	61.94166	26.88028	2.30435	0.02320**	182.33049	85.43090	2.13425	0.03520**
OIL^{-}	124.21280	30.53235	4.06824	0.00010*	36.75849	69.26826	0.53067	0.59680
C	-0.33972	0.07388	-4.59838	0.00000	29710.44688	562.46390	52.82196	0.00000

Before interpreting NARDL results, it is necessary to explain the meaning of asymmetric based coefficients. For a negative NARDL coefficient, negative variations of an explanatory variable imply that when the regressor variable increases, the response variable tends to fall, and vice versa. Again, for a positive coefficient, positive variations of an explanatory variable imply that when the regressor variable rises, the response variable tends to rise. Table 4.4, above, presents the NARDL analysis of the effects of the negative and positive shock of all independent variables on the dependent variable (the US equity market). Positive shocks of IDEMV are negatively significant in both long and short-run periods, while IDEMV are insignificant in cases of negative shock (both long and short-run periods). The coefficient value of $(IDEMV)^{+}$ showed that by increasing IDEMV, the price of the New York stock market decreased dramatically. In other words, the results found that the outbreak of a serious infectious disease brought about negative signals in the equity market, and investors panicked, resulting in decreased performance of the equity market (Baker et al. 2020). Our results exactly match with leverage theory where we found a negative association between equity returns negatively associated with financial asset's volatility. The negative relation is due to investors' behavior totally changing during the period of negative, as compared to positive, news. Similarly, Covid-19 is negatively significant in both negative and positive cases during the short-run period, but the magnitude is high in positive shock, while in the long run, IDEMV is significant only in positive shocks. Our findings are consistent with those of Meninno & Wolf (2020), who pointed out that the Covid-19 virus spread negative news, and increased the vulnerability of the equity market, hindering the performance of the financial market. Lastly, oil is also positively significantly linked with both positive and negative shocks in the short term, while in the long run, IDEMV is significant only in positive shocks. The results are consistent with the previous studies including Smales (2017) which indicated that an increase in oil price enhances equity market performance, while a downward push in the price of oil has an adverse impact on the equity market.

Section 6: Chapter Conclusion

The sharp increase in cases of Covid-19 all over the world has injected a downward trend into the financial equity market. The United States has become the number one country in the world with the highest number of cases and deaths from Covid-19. Therefore, the present study used indexes of oil, US Covid-19, and infectious disease EMV (IDEMV). The recent paper collected the data from 21 January 2020, which was the start of the new coronavirus (Covid-19) in America, up till the present date (6 July 2020). The study used the linear model of autoregressive distributed lag (NARDL) to confirm the causal factors (short-long run) of DJI.

The unit test results depict that the whole chunk of the variables (DJI, US Covid-19, IDEMV, and oil) are stationary at first difference. Moreover descriptive and bound tests also confirm the non-linear co-integration present between the variables of the study. Therefore, the study applies the NARDL model, and results depict that two out the three exogenous (independent) variables (oil, US Covid-19 and infectious disease EMV were significantly negatively related to the United States equity market (DJI) in both positive and negative shocks, except IDEMV, where negative shocks are insignificant. The finding confirms that spreading coronavirus news in the United States and Infectious Disease EMV, hinders the performance of the equity market of the United States. Oil is also significantly positively co-integrated with the DJI index. In the case of long-run co-integration, all variables (oil, US Covid-19, and infectious disease EMV) are significantly co-integrated in cases of positive shocks but insignificantly co-integrated in cases of negative shocks. Our recent study is beneficial for equity investors by pointing out some major reasons for low returns in the United States equity market. In particular, incorporating the infectious disease EMV helps the portfolio find a new uncertainty factor that inversely affects the equity market performance by spreading information asymmetry. So, to diversify their investments, governments and individual investors should to consider these important factors.

References

Al-Awadhi, A. M., Al-Saifi, K., Al-Awadhi, A., &Alhamadi, S. (2020). Death and contagious infectious diseases: Impact of the Covid-19 virus on stock market returns. Journal of Behavioral and Experimental Finance, 100326.

Alqahtani, A., Wither, M. J., Dong, Z., & Goodwin, K. R. (2020). Impact of news-based equity market volatility on international stock markets. Journal of Applied Economics, 23(1), 224-234.

Andrei, D., & Hasler, M. (2015). Investor attention and stock market volatility. The review of financial studies, 28(1), 33-72.

Badeeb, R. A., & Lean, H. H. (2018). Asymmetric impact of oil price on Islamic sectoral stocks. Energy Economics, 71, 128-139.

Baker, S. R., Bloom, N., & Davis, S. J. (2016). Measuring economic policy uncertainty. The quarterly journal of economics, 131(4), 1593-1636.

Baker, S. R., Bloom, N., Davis, S. J., & Kost, K. J. (2019). *Policy news and stock market volatility* (No. w25720). National Bureau of Economic Research.

Baker, S., Bloom, N., Davis, S. J., Kost, K., Sammon, M., & Viratyosin, T. (2020). The unprecedented stock market reaction to Covid-19. *Covid Economics: Vetted and Real-Time P*

Barro, R. J., Ursúa, J. F., & Weng, J. (2020). The coronavirus and the great influenza pandemic: Lessons from the "Spanish flu" for the coronavirus's potential effects on mortality and economic activity (No. w26866). National Bureau of Economic Research.

Black, F. (1976). Studies of stock market volatility changes. 1976 Proceedings of the American Statistical Association Business and Economic Statistics Section.

Bloom, N. (2009). The impact of uncertainty shocks. econometrica, 77(3), 623-685.

Cepoi, C. O. (2020). Asymmetric dependence between stock market returns and news during Covid-19 financial turmoil. Finance Research Letters.

Chen, C. D., Chen, C. C., Tang, W. W., & Huang, B. Y. (2009). The positive and negative impacts of the SARS outbreak: A case of the Taiwan industries. The Journal of Developing Areas, 281-293.

Enamul Hoque, M., Soo Wah, L., & Azlan Shah Zaidi, M. (2019). Oil price shocks, global economic policy uncertainty, geopolitical risk, and stock price in Malaysia: Factor augmented VAR approach. *Economic research-Ekonomskaistraživanja*, *32*(1), 3701-3733.

Epstein, P. R. (2001). West Nile virus and the climate. Journal of Urban Health, 78(2), 367-371.

Fang, L., Qian, Y., Chen, Y., & Yu, H. (2018). How does stock market volatility react to NVIX? Evidence from developed countries. Physica A: Statistical Mechanics and its Applications, 505, 490-499.

Fetzer, T., Hensel, L., Hermle, J., & Roth, C. (2020). Coronavirus perceptions and economic anxiety. arXiv preprint arXiv:2003.03848.

Fleming, J., Ostdiek, B., & Whaley, R. E. (1995). Predicting stock market volatility: A new measure. Journal of Futures Markets, 15(3), 265-302.

Gharib, C., Mefteh-Wali, S., & Jabeur, S. B. (2020). The bubble contagion effect of Covid-19 outbreak: Evidence from crude oil and gold markets. Finance Research Letters, 101703.

Godil, D. I., Sarwat, S., Sharif, A., & Jermsittiparsert, K. (2020). How oil prices, gold prices, uncertainty and risk impact Islamic and conventional

stocks? Empirical evidence from QARDL technique. Resources Policy, 66, 101638.
Hung, N. T. (2019). Equity market integration of China and Southeast Asian countries: further evidence from MGARCH-ADCC and wavelet coherence analysis. Quantitative Finance and Economics, 3(2), 201-220.
Jones, C. M., & Kaul, G. (1996). Oil and the stock markets. The journal of Finance, 51(2), 463-491.
Kumar, S. (2019). Asymmetric impact of oil prices on exchange rate and stock prices. The Quarterly Review of Economics and Finance, 72, 41-51.
Li, K. (2018). Reaction to news in the Chinese stock market: A study on Xiong'an New Area Strategy. Journal of Behavioral and Experimental Finance, 19, 36-38.
Mejova, Y., &Kalimeri, K. (2020). Advertisers Jump on Coronavirus Bandwagon: Politics, News, and Business. arXiv preprint arXiv: 2003.00923.
Meninno, R., & Wolff, G. (2020). As Coronavirus Spreads, Can the EU Afford to Close Its Borders?. Economics in the Time of COVID, 19.
Mo, B., Mu, J., & Zhang, B. (2019). The relationship between news-based implied volatility and volatility of US stock market: What can we learn from multiscale perspective?. Physica A: Statistical Mechanics and its Applications, 526, 121003.
Narayan, P. K., Popp, S., 2010. A new unit root test with two structural breaks in level and slope
Nelson, D. B. (1991). Conditional heteroskedasticity in asset returns: A new approach. Econometrica: Journal of the Econometric Society, 347-370.
Niederhoffer, V. (1971). The analysis of world events and stock prices. The Journal of Business, 44(2), 193-219.
Nikkinen, J., &Peltomäki, J. (2020). Crash fears and stock market effects: evidence from web searches and printed news articles. Journal of Behavioral Finance, 21(2), 117-127.
Nishiura, H., Kobayashi, T., Yang, Y., Hayashi, K., Miyama, T., Kinoshita, R., ... &Akhmetzhanov, A. R. (2020). The rate of under ascertainment of novel coronavirus (2019-nCoV) infection: Estimation using Japanese passengers data on evacuation flights.
Pal, D., & Mitra, S. K. (2015). Asymmetric impact of crude price on oil product pricing in the United States: An application of multiple threshold nonlinear autoregressive distributed lag model. Economic Modelling, 51, 436-443.

Peress, J. (2014). The media and the diffusion of information in financial markets: Evidence from newspaper strikes. The Journal of Finance, 69(5), 2007-2043.

Sadorsky, P. (1999). Oil price shocks and stock market activity. Energy economics, 21(5), 449-469.

Smales, L. A. (2017). The importance of fear: investor sentiment and stock market returns. Applied Economics, 49(34), 3395-3421.

Solomon, D. H. (2012). Selective publicity and stock prices. The Journal of Finance, 67(2), 599-638.

Yin, L., & Feng, J. (2019). Can investors attention on oil markets predict stock returns?. The North American Journal of Economics and Finance, 48, 786-800.

Zheng, Y. (2014). The linkage between aggregate stock market investor sentiment and commodity futures returns. Applied Financial Economics, 24(23), 1491-1513.

Zhu, S., Liu, Q., Wang, Y., Wei, Y., & Wei, G. (2019). Which fear index matters for predicting US stock market volatilities: Text-counts or option based measurement?. Physica A: Statistical Mechanics and its Applications, 536, 122567.

CHAPTER 3

VOLATILITY OF OIL PRICES AND INTERNATIONAL STOCK RETURN

Summary of Chapter Three

The aim of this chapter is to investigate the impact of oil prices on the stock markets of G7 countries. Oil prices not only affect the economy of a country, but also their stock markets. The stock market is directly connected to the stock valuation, or a company's stock value, whereas the stock value is associated with a discounted sum of predictable future cash flows, and these flows may be distressed due to macroeconomic variables in the shape of oil price fluctuations. This study has researched the impact of oil price fluctuation on selected countries, included in the G7, such as Canada, Germany, France, Italy, United Kingdom, United States of America, and Japan. The time period chosen is from September 2009 to August 2016. The most recent data were collected for analysis. In this chapter, the real stock return is considered as a dependent variable, or predictable variable, while oil prices, industrial production, and short-term interest rate, are considered as independent or predictor variables. The study is quantitative in nature, and secondary data has been used for this purpose. Most data has been collected from the OECD website, but oil prices were taken from the oil intelligence report. For the purpose of the chapter, the model used was based on an Arbitrage Pricing Theory (APT) model, in which financial assets are associated with macroeconomic variables. Industrial production is positively associated with a real stock return in the case of Germany, Italy, Japan, United Kingdom and France, while the short-term interest rate is negatively connected with a real stock return in the case of Canada, United Kingdom, and the US. Oil prices insignificantly affected the real stock markets of all countries. The G7 countries included most of the importing countries. Canada joined during the testing of the model.

Keywords: Oil prices, industrial production, and short-term interest rate, real stock return, G7 countries and Arbitrage Pricing Theory-APT model

Section 1: Introduction

Discussions concerning oil prices and their effect have become very common and important in recent times. Much of the literature has observed an association between oil prices and stock markets. Researchers are continuously exploring and finding out the reason for this, as well as the impact of oil fluctuation and how to overcome it, Oil prices not only affect the economy of a country but also its stock market. The stock market is essentially directly connected to the stock valuation, or company's stock value, whereas the stock value is associated with the discounted sum of predictable future cash flows. These flows may be distressed due to macroeconomic variables in the shape of oil price fluctuations. The effects of fluctuation can be positive, negative, or significant which could be discussed further. This research examines the impact of oil prices on the real stock return in G7 (Group of Seven) countries. These countries include both emerging and developed economies. The main research question is how the markets of the above countries respond when the transactional oil price changes.

Generally, if discussing the volatility of oil price fluctuation, the anticipated answer would be that it must be a negative relationship between the stock market and oil prices, as the financial press also view this kind of column. But in reality, it is very complicated to describe, rather than a simple argument. Different series' of examinations have been leading up to catching the influence of oil prices and oil tremors on the economies of development and emerging economies, but research papers which are based on stock markets or stock return exploration are very limited. The results of research by Jones and Huang (1996) to find the impression of oil on the stock market showed no relationship or influence.

The motivation behind writing this chapter is that different studies have been conducted on oil prices since the first shock in 1973. Most of the researchers conducted studies on macroeconomic factors, the reasons for oil price oscillation, the US economy, and the imports and exports of oil countries, but very few papers focus on G7 countries. This chapter will focus on those G7 countries and the way the real market return reacts with oil price oscillation. The aim of the chapter is to describe the stock markets of G7 countries with reference to oil price fluctuation. Previous research will also be considered.

In first section, we discussed the introduction and purpose of the chapter. The second part presents the literature review, which included the different work of researchers in the field of oil prices. The third section related to the statistical methodology of the research, in which the hypotheses, tools, and models which would be used to analyze the collected data are described. Section four is concerned with the detailed testing of the models and selected tools, through which empirical analyses are conducted. Section five is the last, and relates to the final conclusion, recommendations, and potential further research.

Section 2: Literature Review

a. Oil price fluctuation: Concept and historical overview:

i. Background:

In the 1850s, different resources, such as oil from whales and liquor from cultivated crops were extracted from the land. The first crude oil was extracted in 1959 by Col. Drake in Pennsylvania. If we discuss the supply, demand, and price of oil with reference to economic theory, it can be seen that shortages and oversupply of oil are based upon the policies of OPEC and Non-OPEC countries, and not related to demand. The price of oil is, basically, a 'spot price' per barrel which is used as a reference price for buyers and sellers. The spot price of oil is used for grading purposes. It consists of four benchmarks which include:

- West Texas Intermediate (WTI)
- Brent Blend
- Dubai Crude
- OPEC Reference Basket (ORB)

The above oils have their own demand and supply rules, which means that their prices evolve differently. According to the different literature, the major respondents for oil price fluctuation are due to the supply distractions and also due to radical disturbances in the Middle East (Tverberg 2010).

ii. Oil price shocks:

The first literature related to oil price history was written by Hamilton (2010) in his paper on historical shocks. Hamilton focused on the different events which were directly or indirectly related to oil prices. According to the researcher, most worldwide oil price tremors were narrowly interrelated with the clashes which were taking place in the Middle East. Hamilton covered different events, which included World War II, the oil embargo in

1973/1974 and 1978/1979, the Iranian Revolution, the Iran – Iraq war (1980), the Persian war (1990-91) and oil price oscillation factors. It can be easily observed that the value of oil was not as important as it is today. Hamilton argued that as time passed, demand for oil would never be consistent, so variations in price would be possible. Crude oil prices have played a significant part in the global economy, especially in the years 1971, 1979 and 2008.

- **The first oil shock (October 1973 - March 1974)**: In 1973, the Arab- Israeli war when Syria and Egypt fought with Israel, and the US was a financial donor to Israel, presented the main reason for oil crises. In reaction, five of the largest states of Persia and Iran boycotted the supply of oil to the US.
- **The second oil shock (April 1979 – July 1990):** In 1979, the Ayatollah Khomeini came to power in Iran. The impact of this revolution on oil prices was bad, and oil prices were pushed up from \$13 to \$32 per barrel.
- **The first oil counter shock (November 1985 – July 1986):** The first oil counter shock happened when Saudi Arabia cut its level of production by almost 75% to reduce the prices of oil globally. By this action, 25% of prices dropped between 1985 and 1986.
- **The Gulf war (July 1990 - November 1990):** When Iraq launched an assault on Kuwait in 1990, Iraq was supplying 8% of the world's oil. The United Nations banned Iraq's global supply, and Kuwait's production was also completely shut down, which created a shortage in the world market.
- **The Asian financial crisis (January 1997 – December 1998):** Asian financial crises are unpredictable. They also affect oil prices and the production of oil in many countries, both OPEC and Non-OPEC.
- **The third oil shocks (December 2003 - June 2008):** In that period, the price of oil fluctuated from \$16 to \$12 (Marc 2012). This was due to high demand from emerging economies. The third oil shocks were not as difficult to handle for oil-importing countries, because they were much smaller. (Norman-1990).
- **Financial crises (July 2008 - February 2009):** The third oil shocks were considered as boom periods, in which oil prices reached their highest level for the first time. On the other hand, other time periods between July 2008 to February 2009 are also considered as the most significant global financial crises and great recession periods, the great depression of 1930.

- **The fifth oil counter shock (September 2014 - February 2016):** The main reasons for this counter shock was oversupply of oil shale and tar sands, and the global recession, in which prices of oil fell from US$105.79 to US$44, a decrease of 58.4%.

b. Oil prices and economic activity:

According to a large number of previous studies, oil price oscillation has an impact on economic activity mainly through demand and supply. (Bernake 1983). Loungani (1992) argued that oil is a very important part of production processes and manufacturing. If the price of oil increases, costs of production also rise, which ultimately affects the production process. Tatom (1988) discussed that oil prices also have an adverse influence on stock due to growth in organizations' costs. Historically sharp increases or decreases in the price of oil are unpredictable. In reviewing past oil prices, researchers noticed a 76% rise during March 2007 to July 2008. On the other hand, there was a fall of 48% between July 2008 and October 2008. These high percentages of fluctuation in oil prices surely affect the economic activities of any country. According to Arouri (2009), oil prices play a significant role in the economic activities of developed countries.

c. Oil prices and exchange rates:

The exchange rate is a key macroeconomic variable. Sadorky (2001) investigated the relationship between oil prices and emerging stock markets, in which he considered the exchange rate indexes of major currencies, interest rates, oil supply, and world economic activity, as variables. In both methods, stock prices were negatively linked with positive oil shock, while oil price responded positively to a positive emerging market shock. The result of this paper also supports the theory that exchange rate movement is due to the change in oil prices. It also provides evidence of the negative relationship between oil prices and an unexpected increase in oil supply, as well as a positive link with an unexpected increase in demand.

d. Oil prices and oil-exporting countries

Dutch Disease Theory explains the effect of oil price increases with respect to economic growth. This theory was outlined by Neary and Corden in 1982. According to the theory, an industrial structure can change due to an increase in oil prices. Oil-exporting countries must concentrate more on the oil sector, compared to other non-traded sectors. It is suggested that higher oil prices may result in an increase in the local currency value, which automatically increases the level of imported consumer goods, so competition between local producers would be reduced. According to the theory of oil prices, an increase is not fruitful for oil-exporting countries (Sweder 1984).

e. Oil prices and oil-importing countries:

Now we discuss oil-importing countries or oil-dependent countries. Most of the work is conducted by Hamilton, who has discussed the oil dependency of economic activity in various studies. According to several research papers, he argued that there is a strong relationship between oil prices with respect to economic activity and growth. In 1983 there was a negative correlation between oil prices and the economy of the US. Whenever oil prices increased, it created a recession in the US economy, due to its high dependency on oil imports. Economic slowdown was due to the interruption in the supply of oil, which caused a decrease in GDP.

f. Oil prices and the stock market:

In the recent era, links between oil prices and stock markets have been brought to public attention. The reason is that there is persistent exceptional unpredictability in oil prices, which increases uncertainty in the energy sector. When there is uncertainty in the energy sector, it automatically affects the global economy and financial markets. According to the International Monetary Fund (2000), when there is a change in oil prices it also affects economic activity, inflation, and earnings, as well as monetary policy which has implications for the asset prices of companies, and thus, also, the financial markets.

According to the study by Jones and Kaul (1996), a survey on the impact of oil prices on the stock market, conducted by Result, concluded that the North American and Canadian stock prices are rational, because oil prices have a significant impact on current and expected cash flows from both countries. Huang (1996) discussed the different series of channels through which oil prices can affect the stock market, such as the macroeconomic. According to researchers, when oil prices change due to uncertainty, it will have an impact on costs and other variables of production, and the change in the cost of production also influences the stock market or stock prices.

g. Hypothesis development:

This chapter highlights the hypotheses of the research and further data methodology techniques which will be used for analysis:

H1: There is a relationship between real stock market return and oil prices.

H2: There is a relationship between real stock market return and industrial production.

H3: There is a relationship between real stock market return and short term interest rates.

Real stock market return is considered as a dependent variable, and other variables include real oil prices, industrial production and short-term interest rates which are considered as descriptive variables - in accord with the economic system. The same variables were used in the research of Park and Ratii (2007) and Papapetrou (2001).

Section 3: Approaches/Chapter methodology

a. Data collection process:

The data under consideration are all secondary in nature, and collected from different sources. The research study collected the data from September 2009 to August 2016, on a monthly basis. The reason for choosing this period is that they are the most current available for convenient study and consistency.

The first variable is oil prices, which are very important for this study which is being conducted to find the influence of oil prices on the stock market. Data of the oil market was collected from an oil intelligence website. The benchmark which is considered for this study is Brent oil, which is seen as an independent variable. 60% of total world consumption daily is benchmarked by Brent oil. According to Chang (2013) and Park (2008), the significant effect of changes in oil prices can be better analyzed by using Brent. Other variables are the industrial production index and short-term interest rates. Data for both were collected from an OECD website database for G7 countries. They are also considered as independent variables. One more variable which is very important, and is at the base of this study, is stock market return. Data of G7 countries stock indices were collected from the OECD database. For the purpose of real stock market return and real industrial production, the study also considered the Consumer Prices Index for inflation-adjusted proxy. The G7 Consumer Prices Index was accessed through the OECD web database.

i. Statistical tools:

In this study, four main kinds of research analysis will be conducted to estimate the above equation or model.

- Descriptive statistic
- Regression analysis
- Coefficient
- Correlation

The first step defines each selected variable's individual level. In the next step, we move towards regression analysis, in which the study easily identifies the impact of selected variables on the dependent variable. In the next step, the study conducts the F-test to check significance. Further analysis will be conducted on the basis of the coefficient in which the T-test is used to check the significant and insignificant levels of the selected variables. Finally, the last step will be a correlation.

b. The Arbitrage Pricing Theory: APT Model:

The Arbitrage Pricing Theory was presented in 1976 by Stephen Ross. According to this theory, financial assets are linked with different types of macroeconomic variable and these securities are linked by linear function with other variables. Compassion analysis changes in individual variables will be shown in beta. Using the APT, the return is pricing which considers the different macroeconomic variables of the market. On the other hand, using the pricing of stock returns as a dependent macroeconomic variable includes oil prices, interest rates and industrial production, which are used as explanatory variables. Stock return reacts linearly to its symmetry after the change in descriptive variables.

Section 4: Empirical analysis

a. Descriptive statistics of G7 countries:

Table 1 (Appendix A) describes the selected variables with respect to G7 countries. The first variable which needs to be described is the real stock return of the US stock market index from September 2009 to August 2016. A total of 84 observations are included. The next variable is the industrial production index with respect to the US. This index is used to represent the monthly complied changes in the short term in industry overall (Economic Research Centre). The next variable is short-term interest rate with respect to the US. In the short term, Treasury bills and money market rate are usually included. This is a rate which affects short-term borrowing between financial foundations, as can be seen in the government issued paper on the financial market (International Financial Statistics-IFS OECD 2000).

b. Regression analysis:

In Table 2 (Appendix B), the indicator study checks the power of the data. R^2 is the coefficient of determination which pronounces how appropriately the model regression line fits the statistics. It is simply the way the alteration independent variable will be elucidated by the change in independent variables. In the case of Canada's stock return, the value of R^2 is 0.540001518, which is close to the value of 1. This means that about 0.54 of the variation in the real stock return is explained by oil prices, industrial production, and short-term interest rate. The observed value being close to 1 means that the sample regression line fits the data very well.

= F.INV.RT (Probability, Degree of Freedom)
= F.INV.RT (Probability, Regression, Residual)
= F.INV.RT (0.05, 3, 80)
= 2.718784982

In the above table, the value of F is 31.30453912 and the critical value is 2.71. This means that the real stock market has a correlation with other variables. In the case of Germany's stock return, the value of R^2 is 0.017502266, which is close to 0. This means that about 0.01 of the variation in the real stock return is explained by oil prices, industrial production, and short-term interest rate. The observed value is close to 0 which means that the sample regression line does not fit the data very well.

= F.INV.RT (0.05, 3, 80)
= 2.718784982

In the above table, the value of F is 0.47504138, and the critical value is 2.71. This means that the real stock market has no correlation with other variables. The F-test is not successful in the case of Germany.

In the case of Italy's stock return, the value of R^2 is 0.0267175, which is close to 0. It means that about 0.02 of the variation in the real stock return is explained by oil prices, industrial production, and short-term interest rate. An observed value which is close to 0 means that the sample regression line does not fit the data very well.

= F.INV.RT (0.05, 3, 80)
= 2.718784982

In the above table, the value of F is 0.73202462, and the critical value is 2.71. This means that the real stock market has no correlation with other variables. The F-test is not successful in the case of Italy.

In the case of Japan's stock return, the value of R^2 is 0.01991456, which is close to 0. This means that about just 0.01 of the variation in the real stock return is explained by oil prices, industrial production, and short-term interest rate. An observed value which is close to 0 means that the sample regression line does not fit the data very well.

= F.INV.RT (0.05, 3, 80)
= 2.718784982

In the above table, the value of F is 0.5418455, and the critical value is 2.71. This means that the real stock market has no correlation with other variables. The F-test is not successful in the case of Japan.

In the case of the United Kingdom's stock return, the value of R^2 is 0.014398061 which is close to 0. This means that about 0.0.14 of the variation in the real stock return is explained by oil prices, industrial production, and short-term interest rate. An observed value close to 0 means that the sample regression line does not fit the data very well.

= F.INV.RT (0.05, 3, 80)
= 2.718784982

In the above table, the value of F is 0.389557151 and the critical value is 2.71. This means that the real stock market does not correlate with other variables. The F-test is not successful in the case of the United Kingdom.

In the case of the US stock return, the value of R^2 is 0.00317609 which is close to 0. This means that about 0.31 of the variation in the real stock return is explained by oil prices, industrial production, and short-term interest rate. An observed value close to 0 means that the sample regression line does not fit the data very well.

= F.INV.RT (0.05, 3, 80)
= 2.718784982

In the above table, the value of F is 0.08496561, and the critical value is 2.71. This means that the real stock market has no correlation with other variables. The F-test is not successful in the case of the United States of America.

In the case of France's stock return, the value of R^2 is 0.029654053, which is close to 0. This means that about 0.02 of the variation in the real stock return is explained by oil prices, industrial production, and short-term interest rate. An observed value which is close to 0 means that the sample regression line does not fit the data very well.

= F.INV.RT (0.05, 3, 80)
= 2.718784982

In the above table, the value of F is 0.814941046 and the critical value is 2.71. This means that the real stock market has no correlation with other variables. The F-test is not successful in the case of France.

According to Table 3 (Appendix C) of Canada, Germany, Italy, Japan, the UK, the US, and France, the value is significant with respect to the predicted variable. The value of oil prices, industrial production, and interest rate, are all insignificant with respect to real stock return.

Section 5: Conclusion

In recent years, oil prices are among the most discussed topics. This is because, due to changes in oil prices, many developed nations are facing huge losses. On the other hand, they offer opportunities for other developed countries, including oil-importing countries. This research is based on stock market return. How do the selected countries' markets react to a change in oil prices? Of course, it would be difficult to manipulate. To consider previous research articles, this study has shown a limited number of countries for the purpose of correlating oil prices and stock market return. Of course, this study will help investors in investing in G7 nations with respect to changes in oil prices. This study has researched the impact of oil price fluctuation on selected countries which included those in the G7, such as Canada, Germany, France, Italy, the United Kingdom, the United States of America, and Japan. The time periods which were chosen were from September 2009 to August 2016. The most recent data was collected for analysis. In this study, the real stock return was considered as a dependent variable or predictable variable, while oil prices, industrial production, and short-term interest rate, were considered as independent or predictor variables. All data was collected from the OECD website except for oil prices which were taken from an oil intelligence report. Germany, Italy,

France and Japan have a negative association with oil prices. Other selected variables included industrial production and short-term interest rate. Industrial production is positively associated with a real stock return in the case of Germany, Italy, Japan, the United Kingdom and France, while the short-term interest rate is negatively connected with a real stock return in the case of Canada, the United Kingdom, and the US. Oil prices have an insignificant effect on the real stock markets of all countries. The G7 countries include most of the oil-importing countries. During the testing of the model, Canada was accepted.

References

Bernanke, B. S., (1983). "Irreversibility, Uncertainty, and Cyclical Investment." Quarterly Journal of Economics 98, 85-106.

Hamilton, J. D., (2005). "Oil and the Macroeconomy." Forthcoming in Durlauf, S., Blume, L. (Eds), The New Palgrave Dictionary of Economics, 2nd ed., Palgrave MacMillan Ltd.

Huang, R. D., Masulis, R. W., Stoll, H. R., (1996). "Energy shocks and financial markets." Journal of Futures Markets 16, 1-27.

Jones, C. M., Kaul, G., (1996). "Oil and the Stock Market." Journal of Finance 51, 463-491.

Tverberg. (2010). Crude Oil Price, Commodity Prices & Crude Oil Analysis at Oil Price, Retrieved from: http://oilprice.com/Energy

Kim, In-Moo &Loungani, Prakash, (1992). "The role of energy in real business cycle models," Journal of Monetary Economics, Elsevier, vol. 29(2), pages 173-189.

Norman S. (1988). "The International Economy under Stress" Cambridge, Mass.: Ballinger Publishing Co.

Tatom, John A. (1988), "Are the Macroeconomic Effects of Oil Price Changes Symmetric?" Carnegie–Rochester Conference Series on Public Policy 28: 325–68.

Arouri & Fouquau, (2009). "On the short-term influence of oil price changes on stock markets in GCC countries: linear and nonlinear analyses," Economics Bulletin, AccessEcon, vol. 29(2), pages 795-804.

Sadorsky, (2001). "Risk factors in stock returns of Canadian oil and gas companies," Energy Economics, Elsevier, vol. 23(1), pages 17-28.

Corden, W. M. and Neary, J. P. (1982). Booming sector and de-industrialization in a small open economy. The economic journal, 92(368):825–848.

Sweder, (1984). "On Fiscal Deficits, the Real Exchange Rate and the World Rate of Interest," CEPR Discussion Papers 21, C.E.P.R. Discussion Papers.

J. Park, R.A. Ratti, (2008). "Oil price shocks and stock markets in the US and 13 European countries" Energy Economics, 2587-2608

E. Papapetrou, (2001), "Oil price shocks, stock market, economic activity and employment in Greece" Energy Economics. 511-532

Le Tha, H, Chang, Y, (2013), "Oil price shocks and trade imbalances", Energy Economics, Elsevier BV * North-Holland

Stephen A. Ross, (1976), "The Arbitrage Theory of Capital Asset Pricing", Journal of Economic Theory

Appendix A

Table 1: Description of G7 Countries (September 31, 2015 –August 31, 2016)

	CANADA			GERMANY			ITALY			JAPAN		
	RSR	**LNIP**	**IR**	**RSR**	**LNIP**	**IR**	**RSR**	**LNIP**	**IR**	**RSR**	**LNIP**	**IR**
Mean	-0.99	4.664	0.986	-0.000	4.673	0.4682	0.000	4.555	0.467	-0.000	4.579	0.271
Standard Error	3.760	0.004	0.028	0.000	0.005	0.056	0.000	0.004	0.056	0.000	0.003	0.012
Median	-0.99	4.667	1.16	-0.000	4.693	0.3	0.000	4.541	0.3	-0.000	4.582	0.27
SD	0.000	0.044	0.263	0.005	0.055	0.521	0.006	0.039	0.521	0.005	0.032	0.111
SVariance	1.188	0.001	0.069	3.386	0.003	0.271	4.654	0.001	0.272	3.478	0.001	0.012
Kurtosis	1.108	-0.85	0.155	3.593	2.435	-0.574	-0.44	-0.76	-0.58	-0.38	2.781	-0.113
Skewness	0.764	-0.49	-1.20	0.903	-1.78	0.625	0.051	0.739	0.626	0.247	-1.304	0.240
Minimum	-0.99	4.564	0.376	-0.014	4.495	-0.3	0.031	0.140	1.9	-0.013	4.457	0.06
Maximum	-0.99	4.723	1.189	0.025	4.737	1.6	-0.01	4.504	-0.3	0.013	4.629	0.54
Count	84	84	84	84	84	84	0.018	4.644	1.6	84	84	84

	UK			USA			FRANCE		
	RSR	**LNIP**	**IR**	**RSR**	**LNIP**	**IR**	**RSR**	**LNIP**	**IR**
Mean	0.000	4.585	0.653	-0.000	0.263	0.263	-7.474	4.607	0.480
Standard Error	0.000	0.001	0.019	0.000	0.014	0.014	0.000	0.001	0.056
Median	4.858	4.587	0.57	-0.000	0.24	0.24	-9.045	4.606	0.28
Standard Deviation	0.004	0.017	0.179	0.004	0.131	0.131	0.005	0.017	0.518
Sample Variance	1.658	0.000	0.032	1.905	0.017	0.017	3.245	0.000	0.268
Kurtosis	0.066	-0.378	0.394	0.750	0.477	0.477	-0.344	-0.213	-0.617
Skewness	0.167	-0.211	1.225	0.267	1.080	1.080	0.279	0.308	0.613
Minimum	-0.008	4.541	0.47	-0.012	0.11	0.11	-0.011	4.571	-0.29
Maximum	0.009	4.624	1.11	0.011	0.62	0.62	0.016	4.656	1.6
Sum	0.001	389.7	55.58	84	84	84	84	84	84

Appendix B

Table 2: Regression Statistics of G7 Countries

	CANADA	GERMANY	ITALY	JAPAN	UK	USA	FRANCE
Multiple R	0.73484795	0.13229612	0.163454	0.141118	0.1199919	0.056356	0.1722035
R Square	0.54000151	0.01750226	0.026717	0.019914	0.0143980	0.003176	0.0296540
Adjusted R Square	0.52275157	-0.01934139	-0.00978	-0.01683	-0.0225620	-0.034204	-0.006733
Standard Error	0.00023812	0.00587543	0.006855	0.005947	0.0040999	0.004439	0.0057159
F Statistics	31.3045391	0.47504138	0.732024	0.541845	0.3895571	0.084965	0.8149410
Observations	84	84	84	84	84	84	84

Appendix C

Table 3: Countries Stock Return value analysis

	CANADA			**GERMANY**		
	OP	**LNIP**	**IR**	**OP**	**LNIP**	**IR**
P Value	0.074271977	2.48083E-06	0.164243448	0.72559686	0.33298899	0.33276159
	ITALY			**JAPAN**		
	OP	**LNIP**	**IR**	**OP**	**LNIP**	**IR**
P Value	0.98491183	0.33792517	0.33792517	0.33792517	0.3697064	0.50047671
	UK			**USA**		
	OP	**LNIP**	**IR**	**OP**	**LNIP**	**IR**
P Value	0.35905009	0.48788738	0.891075269	0.76015991	0.73638268	0.81934329
	FRANCE					
	OP	**LNIP**	**IR**			
P Value	0.842119538	0.34397682	0.535256008			

CHAPTER 4

ENTREPRENEURSHIP: THE ENGINE OF GROWTH IN EMERGING ECONOMIES

Summary of Chapter Four

This chapter explores educational entrepreneurship programs, which help students in the development of entrepreneurial start-ups. The chapter used a data set from nine universities in three large emerging Asian countries (India, Pakistan, and Bangladesh). The sample size is 837 students, and the study explores whether entrepreneurship education is a suitable means to develop entrepreneurial intention and start-up development. The chapter explores the educational aspects of entrepreneurship (generalized, motivational, and augmented education) and their influence on young graduates' entrepreneurial start-up development. This chapter will be helpful for policymakers to decrease unemployment in society through boosting entrepreneurial education.

Keywords: Cross-Sectional Study, Survey Analysis, Regression Analysis, Entrepreneurial education, Asian countries, entrepreneurial start-up development, society unemployment, educational programs.

Section 1: Introduction

Technology entrepreneurship is one of the topics highlighted in current debates. For the launch and growth of new firms, and their economic development, it is crucial for management and stakeholders to take ideas from markets, engineers, managers, and scientists, to educate and develop entrepreneurial spirit. Entrepreneurship education has been characterized as an essential driver of sustainable socio-economic development (Matlay & Farashah 2013). It plays a significant role in performing productive activities efficiently and effectively, by using commitments, initiatives, and innovative efforts (Acs et al. 2008). Entrepreneurship is mainly all about innovation and creativity in tasks, while entrepreneurship education can be defined as a base for polishing that innovativeness (Molle & Djarova 2009). In specific terms, entrepreneurship education is all about polishing the potential entrepreneurial skills and abilities among graduates, to make them competent when starting their businesses, so that they are capable of flourishing in their careers (Blenker et al. 2014).

In developing countries, the creation of suitable job opportunities for fresh graduates has become a significant issue. Additionally, in the case of traditional university degrees, job opportunities, as well as market demand, may be limited in most cases (Brown 2003). As a result, the rate of unemployment increased as numbers of literate people have continuously increased in the respective countries (Saks & Ashforth 2002). Similarly, many universities produce graduates with quality managerial skills who can fit into any public and private sector organization smoothly, but those organizations are not able to absorb every graduate coming out of the university. As a result, a social and economic imbalance can be created in these countries due to lack of employment opportunities (Okorafor & Okorafor 2011). The present study identified the educational aspects of entrepreneurship (generalized, motivational, and augmented entrepreneurial education) and their influence on young graduates' entrepreneurial start-up development.

The motivation behind the present research is to ensure that universities in emerging economies (India, Pakistan, and Bangladesh) provide their students with entrepreneurship education and help them to develop their intentions of new business start-ups, which will lead to entrepreneurial development in developing nations. As universities in developed nations offer entrepreneurship programs, we identify whether these initiative programs and technology entrepreneurship models can apply in emerging economies. Moreover, what the consequences of this entrepreneurial education would be, and the drawbacks, and what new opportunities are available to students through this model implementation. What are the ways to understand and motivate educational programs in technology entrepreneurship? The reason for the selected cases (India, Pakistan, and Bangladesh) is that these countries are more relevant to the study and have similar economic and social realities. Young graduates are an asset to every country, and encouraging them to start up new enterprises in their careers is a good step to be taken by universities' administrations. These activities encourage them to start up new ventures and make their names in society. Another motivation is that Asian countries, including India, Pakistan, and Bangladesh, are termed as developing economies. One of the significant problems they face is the high unemployment rate prevailing among graduates passing out each year from institutions of higher education. The primary reason for this is the preference of graduates for becoming paid employees in organizations, instead of engaging themselves in self-employment (Muszafarsha & Woon 2004, Fong 2005). We aim to verify that generalized, motivational and augmented entrepreneurial education in universities significantly influences entrepreneurial startup development, and show how these programs develop the intentions of university graduates towards innovative technological startup ventures in emerging economies (India, Pakistan, and Bangladesh).

This chapter is divided into four parts. The second part will explain the background/critical analysis and literature review, which includes theoretical support, an explanation of university entrepreneurial education programs, and their impact on entrepreneurial startup development. The third part explains the approaches and methodologies, the fourth part will provide empirical research analysis, and the fifth part concludes with its practical implication in today's technology-changed environment.

Section 2: Literature Review

2.1. Basic entrepreneurship concept

The word 'entrepreneurship' originates from a French word, 'entrepreneur' which describes an individual who undertakes any initiative by him/herself. Muller & Korsgaard (2018) also discussed entrepreneurship and its role and context. The term 'entrepreneur' describes an individual who has the ability to explore every new opportunity to incorporate innovative, beneficial ideas of value into a variety of actions, including use of personal time, resources, efforts, and individual skills or capabilities, to make a business successful in the marketplace. In other words, the entrepreneur is the one who tackles business risks effectively and efficiently (Kuratko & Hodgetts 2009).

2.2. Entrepreneurship theories and models

There is a need for strong theoretical support for entrepreneurship development. There are several theories which support the concept of entrepreneurship education and its development. Some fundamental theories are given below:

a) Theory of planned behavior:

The theory of planned behavior, by Ajzen and Fishbein (1980) was classified as one of the most popular entrepreneurship theories for students. The modified theory of planned behavior is a theory of reasoned action given by Sheppard et al. (1988) who stated that our every action is based on some intention or reason (Shapero 1982, Krueger 1993). This theory explained that the intention of entrepreneurship stems from the perception of desirability and feasibility of a person, and this relation is affected by social and cultural context. This model holds some variables of attitude towards behavior and perceived behavior control which are affected by subjective norms (Turker et al. 2009). These attitudes and social norms have a more significant impact on student intentions of entrepreneurship, which causes motivational behavior towards new ventures (Autio, Keeley, Klofsten, Parker & Hay 2001).

b) Theory of Achievement:

One of the most accepted theories on entrepreneurship development among students is the Theory of Achievement, provided by McClelland in 1961. Individuals who had a strong need for achievement performed better and were engaged in more challenging and innovative tasks. These individuals look for improved ways of achievement, success, and a higher level of performance (Utsch & Rauch 2000, Littunen 2000). According to McClelland's theory, moderate risk is needed in the initial stages of a business. It is important that an individual is a moderate risk taker, pays attention to the supervisory response of profit and cost, assumes personal responsibility, and finds innovative and creative ways to develop new products and services. The theory also states that those characteristics prevail in individuals who have a high need for motivation and achievement (Raposo, do Paco & Ferreira 2008). McClelland's theory of achievement shows a unique type of 'entrepreneurship personality' which includes the needs for affiliation, power, and achievement.

2.3. Developments in Entrepreneurship History

The roots and early expansion of the concept of entrepreneurship were traced back to the 18th century, when a French economist, Richard, firstly coined the word 'entrepreneur'. The entrepreneur was described as one who introduced a new product and service in the marketplace by utilizing all available means of production (Schumpeter 1951). The concept was studied by British economists, who described entrepreneurship as the management of the business (Burnett 2000). Alfred Marshall (1994), emphasized the importance of entrepreneurship for production purposes, and thus presented the concept of four factors of production; namely land, labor, capital, and organization. Logical evolution of these concepts has been continuously observed in entrepreneurship, and thus the idea of entrepreneurship has emerged as one of the significant organizational driving forces which effectively coordinate all factors of production effectively in the marketplace for achieving desired organizational outcomes (Coulter 2003).

Moreover, entrepreneurship has also been characterized as essential for positive economic growth (Burnett 2000). Additionally, various researchers from multiple disciplines have described the characteristics of entrepreneurs differently. The famous economists Kirzner (1985) and Alfred Marshall (1994) stated that the entrepreneur is an individual who has specific capabilities and skills that translate into innovative products, services, and businesses. A plethora of studies in entrepreneurship have also termed entrepreneurs as innovative individuals. Li, Qu & Huang (2017) explained the graduated behavior of innovative new venture start-ups, and they state that this behavior could occur through students' psychological factors, such as self-efficacy, overconfidence, and so forth. In short, distinctive characteristics were found to exist among entrepreneurs both in developed and developing countries, promoting entrepreneurship as the process of creative and innovative imagination (Burnett 2000, Katz 2003, Kuratko 2005).

2.4. Entrepreneurship development in emerging countries2

There are various countries in which entrepreneurship is considered one of the principal subjects to teach students. However, in some countries, there is a need to encourage and focus on this crucial phenomenon. There are some emerging countries of Asian regions who are trying to enhance their students' abilities through entrepreneurship education, and there is a need to place more focus on this matter, to overcome poverty and unemployment in emerging economies.

a) Entrepreneurship education in Pakistan:

In Pakistan, the education of entrepreneurship is still an unfamiliar discipline. It needs a more significant focus from the Higher Education Commission. According to William & Shahid (2016), the young generation in Pakistan acts while choosing their entrepreneurship career, and they have no support from their institutions. More than a decade back, the HEC realized the importance of entrepreneurship education with changing global trends and considered including this education in the coursework of students. However, this subject is still limited to one or two courses in postgraduate and undergraduate degree programs in business administration (Muhib & Khan 2010).

b) Entrepreneurship education in India:

In India, most universities and business schools offer their students entrepreneurship education which enhances the full range of skills, and use multidisciplinary approaches for their mature students. However, considering this course as a fundamental management subject is essential for the students, alongside other marketing, courses such as HRM. This initiative develops unique solutions to satisfy customers' needs and will be helpful to promote entrepreneurship education as a core and fundamental way to enhance business education in Indian institutions (Basu 2014).

c) Entrepreneurship education in Bangladesh:

In Bangladesh, entrepreneurship development courses are offered at MBA and BBA levels in different private and public-sector universities. These courses provide a medium level of effectiveness in the country. There is a need to focus on this subject in Bangladeshi universities. The modest level of economic growth in Bangladesh, reduced level of industrialization, and large unemployment level, show that Bangladeshi universities are not making significant headway in entrepreneurship development. So, there is a need for entrepreneurship education and training (Azim & Akbar 2010).

2.5. Entrepreneurial startup development

The younger generation is significant for any country; it is an asset and young people need proper training and education to make their future bright. The time of adolescence, when students begin to acquire a confident attitude and attain knowledge, is also their graduation time, and it's crucial for young people to understand their career requirements. It is vital for the universities and schools to encourage the students to take part in entrepreneurial activities which shape their beliefs (Filion 1994) and contribute to enhancing their inherent abilities and attention towards entrepreneurial opportunities (Young 1997, Kourilsky 1995). Entrepreneurship education and intentions encourage students' entrepreneurial startup development. Through this process, entrepreneurs can start up their new businesses. These programs develop entrepreneurs' initiatives and ideas, and provide students with high potential opportunities, helping them to develop their own entrepreneurship ideas, to sell their new business marketing plans, and manage rapid growth. These new business startups in turn, help and develop entrepreneurship in emerging economies.

2.6. Definition of Entrepreneurship Education and its Chronology

The primary variable is entrepreneurship education and its encouragement. Entrepreneurship education is defined as the entire educational system; a full set of training and education activities. Entrepreneurship education is one of the methods through which universities can encourage their students to think 'out of the box', and it is an activity which creates graduates' intentions to engage in entrepreneurial behavior. There are some factors which profoundly influence entrepreneurs, including activities, desirability, knowledge, and feasibility (Linan 2004). Katz developed the chronology of entrepreneurship education in 2003, but the concept dates back to 1876, with agricultural and economic literature, and it was included in hardware course literature in 1947. At the business school of the University of South California, entrepreneurship education was offered in 1970, with the launch of their new MBA program. After a while this course became an enormous success, and by early 1980 it was included in 300 university entrepreneurship programs. By 1990 the number of these courses grew to 1050, in 2000 universities and colleges around the globe (Charney & Libecap 2000). For entrepreneurs, the continuous increase in entrepreneurial education as a field of study through the rational and integration approach gained popularity around the world (Zeithaml & Rice 1987).

2.7. Aspects of graduate entrepreneurship intention

Young graduates are an asset of every country and helping them to start up new enterprises for their career is a good step taken by universities. These activities encourage them to start up new ventures and make their names in society. This step is also useful in the eradication of poverty among youth, as new ventures help decrease unemployment, and empower the country to fight against economic recession. There are diverse situational factors quoted in earlier articles that may affect the intentions of individuals toward activities related to entrepreneurship careers. A more detailed examination of the recent financial crisis (an economic recession) is needed. This recession may have an impact on the decision of an individual to engage in entrepreneurial activities. It is needed especially in nations who deeply felt the implications of the crisis, such as Greece. Entrepreneurship education started years ago, but many researchers have stated that this field is emergent and in the phase of adolescence. The lack of theories and paradigms accepted in entrepreneurship literature education has been stressed by many entrepreneurship authors (Fiet 2000, Kuratko 2005). Universities can play a leading role in creating and motivating students and driving their behavior towards entrepreneurship development (Linan 2004a, 2004b). There are different entrepreneurship education programs and efforts which contribute significantly to entrepreneurship development, including generalized entrepreneurial education, motivational entrepreneurial education, and augmented entrepreneurial education.

2.8. Description of study variables

a) Generalized entrepreneurial education:

This intends to identify the vibrant and useful potential in everyone. The purpose of generalized entrepreneurial education is to provide a student learning outcome that can be valued in the real world (Fayolle 2007). This type of learning creates an impression that encourages students to relate their former principles and theory of knowledge, and at the same time, develops their commitment to practice and gives them experience which helps them to understand whether their achieved results are successes or failures (Löbler 2006).

b) Motivational entrepreneurial education:

When people feel competent and self-determined in work, their motivation rises (Deci and Ryan 2000). Motivational entrepreneurship education motivates an individual to choose entrepreneurship as his/her passion and as his/her career. Entrepreneurship is not considered by young people at the preliminary stages of their careers (Fishbein and Ajzen 2010, Ronstadt 1985). Through the motivational speeches related to entrepreneurship development and motivation, education encourages the student to 'think outside the box' and show the skills to start their enterprises. Motivation persuades the entrepreneur to assess, search for, and make use of, opportunities available (Shane et al. 2003, Fishbein and Ajzen 2010). This motivational entrepreneurship education is considered to be the most critical determinant which links entrepreneurship intention and action.

c) Augmented entrepreneurial education:

The focus of augmented entrepreneurship is self-efficacy. A variety of factors including feasibility studies, case study competitions, and business plans are the major factors for self-efficacy development among students, and are seen as the essential requirements for entrepreneurship development among students at university level (Wilson et al. 2007). Self-efficacy can be defined as the capabilities of an individual for organizing and executing a specific course of action to tackle a situation (Bandura 1995). Similarly, the self-system is the combination of attitudes, abilities, and cognitive skills of an individual. Additionally, the self-system is seen as necessary because of its reflection of an individual's feeling about any specific situation, as well as the behavior of that individual about various distinct situations.

In short, besides general entrepreneurial education and motivational entrepreneurial education, augmented entrepreneurial education is also critical to build self-efficacy and self-system among students at university level, and is considered as a vital requirement for entrepreneurship development among university level students (Wilson et al. 2007).

2.9. Theoretical base and relationship analysis

a) Influence of generalized entrepreneurial education and entrepreneurship development

In past times, it was widely believed that entrepreneurial qualities are inherently embedded within an individual at birth, rather than being developed at a later stage through entrepreneurial education in the field (Gnyawali & Fogel 1994). Nowadays, this trend has been significantly changed. Researchers in entrepreneurship are of the view that entrepreneurship education at university level can enhance entrepreneurship qualities among individuals.

Moreover, entrepreneurship education has enabled the creation of certain new traits of entrepreneurship among individuals (Henderson & Robertson 2000). Past studies consistently reported that entrepreneurial qualities exist inherently in each and every human being. In other words, the potential of entrepreneurship exists in every individual (Wilson et al. 2009). Hence, positive entrepreneurial attitudes and behaviors can be developed among students towards small and medium enterprises business by focusing effectively on entrepreneurial education at university, especially in developing economies (Solomon 2007, Wilson 2008). Thus, business students taking courses in entrepreneurial education usually avoid starting their careers as employees of specific organizations. They prefer start-ups and the establishment of new business enterprises on their own, compared to seeking employment in any organization in the marketplace (Owusu–Ansah 2012). Students' interest in entrepreneurship can be developed and encouraged significantly by focusing on entrepreneurship education at university level, which translates into a certain level of entrepreneurship development (Wilson et al. 2007).

Hypothesis 1: Generalized entrepreneurial education will be positively associated with entrepreneurial startup development among students at university level.

b) Influence of motivational entrepreneurial education and entrepreneurship development

In today's turbulent business environment, entrepreneurship has not traditionally been considered as the first choice of career by recently graduated students (Ronstadt 1985). Past studies consistently argued that there is a need to develop self-determination among individuals at university level, to motivate them to start up their new businesses after completion of their education (Shane et al. 2003). It is widely believed that the attitudes of individuals can be shaped towards entrepreneurship, as individuals follow the approved behaviors of successful mentors, in both positive and negative circumstances which vary over time. Hence, it is argued that an individual intention to pursue entrepreneurship as a career can be influenced by interacting with entrepreneurs in a related area (Li et al. 2008).

Moreover, providing a platform for the interaction of students with mentors and entrepreneurs at university level positively contributes towards the development of entrepreneurship among students. Additionally, along with the motivation by educational institutions of students for pursuing entrepreneurship as a career, the decisions of an individual to become an entrepreneur is also encouraged and promoted by parents, as motivational entrepreneurial parents also positively contribute towards the development of entrepreneurship (Lee et al. 2005). As a result, motivational entrepreneurship education of students at university level is seen as significant as it links the entrepreneurship intentions of graduates with the required actions, and thus persuades them to explore and use the available entrepreneurship opportunities in the market place (Shane et al. 2003).

Hypothesis 2: Motivational entrepreneurial education will be positively associated with entrepreneurial startup development among students at university level.

c) Influence of augmented entrepreneurial education and entrepreneurship development

Self-efficacy is another requirement for entrepreneurship (Wilson et al. 2007). Bandura (1995) explained self-efficacy/augmented entrepreneurship education as a belief in a person's capabilities to execute and organize a course of action which is required to manage the situation prevailing in the organization. He stated that the role of community experience, observational learning, and determinism on a mutual basis could contribute to individual personality. Further, he asserted that a person's abilities, cognitive skills, and attitude, make up what that self-system is. This self-efficacy system plays a pivotal role in identifying how individuals perceive various situations, and how they behave in response. For developing a person's self-system and self-efficacy, augmented entrepreneurship education is needed, along with motivational and generalized entrepreneurial education. Though motivational and general entrepreneurial education has a positive impact on the development of entrepreneurship, many studies stated that very few students focus on their careers as entrepreneurs by taking courses on entrepreneurship at a graduate level. Ronstadt (1985) explained that motivational and generalized entrepreneurship education is not enough on its own for entrepreneurship development. Some augmented level of entrepreneurship education is also needed. Against this background in entrepreneurship education for entrepreneurship development among students at university level, augmented entrepreneurial education is characterized as another integral aspect of entrepreneurship education for achieving the desired outcomes, of developing entrepreneurial intentions among students at university level. Universities should arrange some creative educational programs, such as opportunity seeking, creative problem-solving programs, group leadership, community cooperation, dealing with bureaucracy, and presentation skills, alongside traditional education, which will lead students to enhance their intentions toward entrepreneurship (Marques and Albuquerque 2012).

Hypothesis 3: Augmented entrepreneurial education will be positively associated with entrepreneurial startup development among students at university level.

Section 3: Research Methodology

We have identified nine leading universities: The Indian Institute of Technology, Delhi (IITD), the University of Delhi, and the University of Calcutta, Quaid-i-Azam University in Islamabad, Fatimah Jinnah University in Rawalpindi, and the Islamic University in Islamabad, and the University of Dhaka, Chittagong University, and North South University in Bangladesh. 100 questionnaires were issued in each university, creating a good empirical representation. The total sample set was 900, and identification and the treatments were random. The response rate was 93%, i.e. 837 respondents filled out the questionnaire. The time horizon selected is cross-sectional, at one point in time in 2017. The statistical technique used for the study was Andrew F. Hayes' PROCESS technique which is an extension of SPSS software, and structured questionnaire for analysis. The sampling technique was the non-probability sampling technique of convenience sampling. Reliability analysis shows that all variables were reliable and correct; for all variables Cronbach's Alpha value was more than 70% which shows that the items were reliable, and can be used for further analysis. The questionnaire asked for some demographic/personal information about students which is also explained in Table 1, which shows that respondents were more male than female, with males representing 58% and females 42%. More students were from the age groups of 21 to 30 and 31 to 40, as their percentages were 37.2% and 36.9% respectively, which shows that more students belonged to the age group of 21-30 years. The percentage of students doing Masters' degrees in the selected universities was 43.8%. The University of Dhaka from Bangladesh students' response rate was higher than other universities (Table 1).

Section 4: Evidence and Analysis

Reliability analysis was conducted to check whether the data is accurate, consistent, and reliable in nature. According to Gerber and Finn (2005) a Cronbach's Alpha value equal to, or greater than, 0.6 indicates that the scale used for data collection purposes is reliable and consistent in nature. The alpha value of augmented entrepreneurship education was 0.818 which showed that the data is consistent. The motivational and generalized entrepreneurship education items' alpha values were 0.613 and 0.787 respectively, which were again, higher than 0.6 and showed that the scales used for motivational and generalized entrepreneurship education were consistent and reliable in nature (Table 2). All variables' Cronbach's Alpha values were greater than 0.6 which showed that all items were reliable for further analysis purposes. Validity analysis was conducted to determine that the weather data was valid, and to find out whether a common method bias existed. Any variable load of 2 or 3 factors shows that data is not valid and there are different dimensions of variable. The percentage of variance should be less than 50%, and the Eigen value should be >1 for validity analysis. If the Eigen value is greater than one and variance is greater than 50%, it means that there is an issue of 'common method variance'. In the present study, the Eigen value was >1 and the percentage of variance was less than 50% so there was no common method bias issue.

The correlation analysis shows how much variables depend on each other, while regression analysis shows how much change a one-unit shift in the independent variable can cause. Table 3 gives some useful test results used to confirm our hypothesis. The correlation analysis shows the variable co-dependency. The SPSS analysis shows the mean and standard deviation of variables firstly. The correlation value should be less than 0.80; if it exceeds the limit, variables dependency is also increased. The correlation between motivational entrepreneurial education and generalized entrepreneurial education is 0.445, which is a moderate correlation between both variables and shows no co-dependency. The correlation between augmented entrepreneurial education, generalized entrepreneurial education, and motivational entrepreneurial education is 0.378 and 0.365 respectively, which shows a weak correlation between variables. Moreover, the last result is the entrepreneurial startup development correlation with other independent variables, the result is less than 0.6 which shows a moderate correlation among variables. So overall, it is stated that no single variables correlation is higher than 0, which indicates that variables are not correlated with each other, and there is no standard method bias arising between variables. The correlation analysis results show that there is no association between variables, and all variables act independently.

4.1 Regression analysis

Regression analysis shows how many independent variables (generalized entrepreneurial education, motivational entrepreneurial education, and augmented entrepreneurial education) have an impact on the dependent variable (entrepreneurial startup development). The regression model is given below:

Entrepreneurial Startup Development= $\alpha + \beta_1$ (Generalized Entrepreneurial Education) + β_2 (Motivational Entrepreneurial Education) + β_3 (Augmented Entrepreneurial Education) + e (i)

The Durbin Watson test (DWT) is used to test autocorrelation of independent variables, and to minimize the correlation of error term. Its value must be less than 3. In this study, the DWT value is less than 3, which shows that no autocorrelation exists between independent variables. Entrepreneurial education has a significant impact on entrepreneurial startup development (See Table 3). Their values are 0.004, 0.001, and 0.000 respectively, which are less than 0.05 ($P < 0.05$). The T values of variables are positive, which shows that generalized, motivational and augmented entrepreneurial education positively affects entrepreneurial startup development. The R square value shows how much change in the dependent variable is caused by one-unit changes in the independent variable. A one-unit change in generalized, motivational and augmented entrepreneurial education causes 0.447, 0.574, 0.544 change in entrepreneurial startup development, respectively.

The beta value of variables shows how strong the relationship between the variables is. The beta value of generalized entrepreneurial education value is 0.458, which shows that a 0.458 (or 45.8%) strong relationship exists between generalized entrepreneurial education and entrepreneurial startup development. The beta value of motivational entrepreneurial education is 0.578, which shows that a 0.578 (or 57.8%) strong relationship exists between motivational entrepreneurial education and entrepreneurial startup development. The best value of augmented entrepreneurial education is 0.541, which shows a 0.541 (or 54.1%) strong relationship exists between augmented entrepreneurial education and entrepreneurial startup development. The VIF value should be less than 10; its values are 2.147, 3.098 and 2.445 which shows that the data is not co-linear. As the beta value is positive, this shows a positive impact of entrepreneurial education in universities on entrepreneurial startup development.

Section 5: Chapter Conclusion

This chapter's purpose was to identify different entrepreneurial education programs which can help to generate students' intentions regarding entrepreneurial activities, which will then lead towards entrepreneurial startup development. We collected data from nine universities in India, Pakistan, and Bangladesh; three universities from each country, on a convenience sampling basis. We found that a positive and meaningful relationship exists between generalized entrepreneurial education, motivational entrepreneurial education, and augmented entrepreneurial education and entrepreneurial startup development. Also, motivational entrepreneurship education has a more significant impact on the dependent variable than the other two educational programs. We recommend that universities should offer new entrepreneurship programs and courses, and use the motivational technique for their students, indicating that when a person feels competent and self-determined in work, his/her motivation rises. Findings will be helpful for policymakers, such as higher education commissions, to enhance the entrepreneurial education in their institutions through different motivational programs, offer students entrepreneurship courses in their semester coursework, and initiate them into their new businesses which, in turn, can be helpful to decrease unemployment rates in their countries. Governments should also initiate the students by giving them interest-free loans, and encouraging them to make entrepreneurship their career.

References

Azim MT, Akbar MM. 2010.Entrepreneurship Education in Bangladesh: A Study Based on Program Inputs. South Asian Journal of Management. 17(4)

Acs ZJ, Desai S, Hessels J. 2008. Entrepreneurship, economic development and institutions", Small Business Economics. 31(3): 219-234.

Ajzen I, Fishbein M, 1980. Understanding Attitudes and Predicting Social behavior. Prentice-Hall, Englewood Cliffs. New Jersey.

Autio E. Keeley RH, Klofsten M, Ulfstedt T. 1997. Entrepreneurial intent among students: testing an intent model in Asia. Enterprise and Innovation Management Studies. 2(2):145-160.

Basu R. 2014.Entrepreneurship Education in India: A Critical Assessment and a Proposed Framework. Technology Innovation Management Review.

Blenker P, Trolle ES, Hedeboe FS, Korsgaard S, Wagner K. 2014. Methods in entrepreneurship education research: a review and integrative framework. Education + Training. 56(8/9):697-715.

Brown P. 2003. The opportunity trap: education and employment in a global economy. European Educational Research Journal. 2(1):141-179.

Burnett D. 2000. The Supply of Entrepreneurship and Economic Development. www.Technopreneurial.com.

Bandura A. 1995. Self-Efficacy in Changing Societies, Cambridge University Press. New York. NY.

Charney A, Libecap GD. 2000. Impact of entrepreneurship education', Insights: A Kauffman research series. Kansas City. MO: Kauffman Center for Entrepreneurial Leadership.

Coulter M K. 2003. Entrepreneurship in action. 2nd Edition. Prentice Hall, Upper Saddle River, N.J.

Deci EL, Ryan RM. 2000. 'The' what' and 'why' of goal pursuits: human needs and the self-determination of behavior. Psychological Inquiry. 11(4):227-268.

Fayolle A. 2007. Handbook of Research in Entrepreneurship Education – A General Perspective. volume 1, Cheltenham (UK): Edward Elgar.

Fiet JO. 2000a. The theoretical side of teaching entrepreneurship. Journal of Business Venturing, 16(1):1-24.

Fishbein M, Ajzen I. 2010. Prediction and Change of Behavior: The Reasoned Action Approach, Psychology Press, New York, NY.

Filion LJ. 1994. Ten steps to entrepreneurial teaching. Journal of Small Business and Entrepreneurship, 11(3):68-78.

Gnyawali DR, Fogel DS. 1994. Environments for entrepreneurship development: key dimensions and research implications. Entrepreneurship Theory and Practice. 18(4):43-62.

Henderson R, Robertson M. 2000. Who wants to be an entrepreneur? Young adult attitudes to entrepreneurship as a career. Career Development International. 41(5):279-287.

Harry MP, Dehghanpour FA. 2013. The process of impact of entrepreneurship education and training on entrepreneurship perception and intention: studyof educational system of Iran. Education+ Training. 55(8/9):868-885.

Kuratko DF, Hodgetts RM. 2009. Entrepreneurship: Theory, Process and Practice. 8thedn.Thomson Learning, Ohio, US.

Kruger ME. 2004. Creativity in the entrepreneurship domain. Ph.D. thesis, Department of Business Management, University of Pretoria.

Kourilsky ML. 1995. Entrepreneurship education: opportunity in search of curriculum. paper presented at the Business Education Forum, October.

Kirzner IM. 1985. Discovery and the Capitalist Process. Chicago: University of Chicago Press.

Kuratko DF. 2005. The emergence of entrepreneurship education: development, trends and challenges. Entrepreneurship Theory and Practice, 29(5):577-597

Littunen H. 2000. Entrepreneurship and the characteristics of the entrepreneurial personality. International Journal of Entrepreneurial Behavior & Research. 6(6):295-309.

Lee SM, Chang D, Lim SB. 2005. Impact of entrepreneurship education: a comparative study of the US and Korea. The International Entrepreneurship and Management Journal, 1(1):27-43.

Li J, Wu S, Wu L. 2008. The impact of higher education on entrepreneurial intentions of university students in China. Journal of Small Business and Enterprise Development. 15(4):752-774.

Li J, Qu J, Huang Q. 2017. Why are some graduate entrepreneurs more innovative than others? The effect of human capital, psychological factor and entrepreneurial rewards on entrepreneurial innovativeness. Entrepreneurship & Regional Development (An International Journal). 1-23

Linan F, 2004a. Education empresarial y modela de intenciones. Formacion para un Empresariado de calidad. Ph.D. dissertation, Dpto, Economia Aplicada I, Universidad de Sevilla, Sevilla.

Löbler H. 2006. Learning entrepreneurship from a constructivist perspective. Technology Analysis & Strategic Management. 18(1):19-38.

Muhib Y, Khan NA. 2010. The Prospects of Entrepreneurial Education in Pakistan: An Economic Perspective. Journal of Independent Studies and Research-Management, Social Sciences and Economics, 8(2)

Muller S, Korsgaard S. 2018. Resources and bridging: the role of spatial context in rural entrepreneurship. Entrepreneurship & Regional Development (An International Journal). 30(1-2)

Molle W, Djarova J. 2009. Enhancing the Effectiveness of Innovation: New Roles for Key Players, Edward Elgar Publishing, Cheltenham.

Marques LA, Albuquerque C. 2012. Entrepreneurship education and the development of young people's life competencies and skills. ACRN Journal of Entrepreneurship Perspectives, 1(2):55-68.

McClelland DC. 1976. The Achievement Motive'. New York, Irvington

Okorafor P, Okorafor A. 2011. Reappraising technical and vocational education and training (TVET) for functionality and self-reliance. Journal of Qualitative Education. 7(1):80-87.

Owusu-Ansah W. 2012. Entrepreneurship education, a panacea to graduate unemployment in Ghana? International Journal of Humanities and Social Science, 2(15):211-220.

Raposo M, Paco A, Ferreira J. 2008. Entrepreneur's profile: taxonomy of attributes and motivations of university students. Journal of Small Business and Enterprise Development, 15(2):405-418.

Ronstadt R. 1985. Every entrepreneur's nightmare: the decision to become an ex-entrepreneur and work for someone else. Frontiers of Entrepreneurship Research 1985 Proceedings of the Fifth Annual

Babson College Entrepreneurship Research Conference. Wellesley, MA:409-434.

Saks AM, Ashforth BE. 2002. Is job search related to employment quality? It all depends on the fit. Journal of Applied Psychology. 87(4):646-654.

Sheppard BH, Hartwick J, Warshaw PR. 1988. The theory of reasoned action: a metaanalysis of past research with recommendations for modifications and future research. J Cons Res, 15(3):325–343.

Shapero A. 1972. The process of technical company formation in a local area. In A C Cooper & J L. Dyer, W G, Jr. 1992. The entrepreneurial experience'. San Francisco: Jossey Bass.

Shane S, Locke EA, Collins CJ. 2003. Entrepreneurial motivation. Human Resource Management Review. 13(2):257-279.

Schumpeter Joseph A. 1951. Economic Theory and Entrepreneurial History', in R V Clemence, ed. Essays on Economic Topics of Joseph Schumpeter. Port Washington, NY: Kennikat Press.

Solomon G. 2007. An examination of entrepreneurship education in the United States. Journal of Small Business and Enterprise Development. 14(2):168-182.

Turker D, Selcuk SS. 2009. Which factors affect entrepreneurial intention of university students. Journal of European Industrial Training, 33(2):142-159.

Utsch A, Rauch A. 2000. Innovativeness and initiative as mediators between achievement orientation and venture performance. European Journal of Work and Organisational Psychology, 9(1):45-62.

William CC, Shahid MS. 2016. Informal entrepreneurship and institutional theory: explaining the varying degrees of (in)formalization of entrepreneurs in Pakistan. Entrepreneurship & Regional Development, (An International Journal),26

Wilson F, Kickul J, Marlino D. 2007. Gender, entrepreneurial self-efficacy, and entrepreneurial career intentions: implications for entrepreneurship education1. Entrepreneurship Theory and Practice. 31(3):387-406.

Wilson KE. 2008. Entrepreneurship Education in Europe. Entrepreneurship and Higher Education,OCED, available at http://ssrn.com/abstract=1392369.

Wilson KE, Vyakarnam S, Volkmann C, Mariotti S, Rabuzzi D. 2009. Educating the next wave of entrepreneurs-unlocking entrepreneurial capabilities to meet the global challenges of the 21st century: a report of the global education initiative. World Economic Forum, Geneva.

Young JE. 1997. Entrepreneurship education and learning for university students and practicing entrepreneurs. in Sexton, D L, Smilor, R W

(Eds), Entrepreneurship 2000, Upstart Publishing, Chicago, IL, pp.215-242.
Zeithaml CP, Rice GH. 1987. Entrepreneurship/Small business education in American universities. Journal of Small Business Management. 25(1):44–50.

Table 1: Demographic Profile of Sample

Questions	Options	Frequency	Percent	Mean	Standard Deviation
Gender	Male	485	57.9	1.753	0.431
	Female	352	42.0		
Age	Below 20	113	13.5	1.804	0.910
	21-30	312	37.2		
	31-40	309	36.9		
	41& above	103	12.3		
Program	Undergraduate	289	34.5	3.167	1.079
	Master	367	43.8		
	Doctoral	83	9.9		
	Diploma	98	11.7		
University (Country)	Quaid-i-Azam University	94	11.2	1.678	0.731
	Islamabad	95	11.3		
	Fatimah Jinnah University				
	Rawalpindi	92	10.9		
	Islamic University Islamabad	89	10.6		
	Indian Institute of	93	11.1		
	Technology Delhi	92	10.9		
	University of Delhi	98	11.7		
	University of Calcutta	93	11.1		
	University of Dhaka	91	10.8		
	Chittagong University				
	North South University				

Table 2: Reliability Analysis

Variables	No of items	Cronbach Alpha
Generalized Entrepreneurship Education	7	0.818
Motivational Entrepreneurship Education	3	0.613
Augmented Entrepreneurship Education	6	0.787
Entrepreneurship Development	6	0.697

Source: Developed by Researcher (2018)

Table 3: Correlation analysis

Variables	Mean	S.D.	GEE	MEE	AEE	ETD
Generalized Entrepreneurial Education	1.906	0.639	1			
Motivational Entrepreneurial Education	1.909	0.553	0.445*	1		
Augmented Entrepreneurial Education	2.005	0.673	0.378*	0.365*	1	
Entrepreneurial start-up Development	1.929	0.611	0.577*	0.526*	0.539*	1

*Correlation is significant at the 0.01 (99%) level, **Correlation is significant at the 0.05 (95%) level, ***Correlation is significant at the 0.10 (90%) level

Table 4: Regression Analysis

Variables	Un-standardized Coefficient Beta	Standardized Coefficient Beta	R^2	T	Sig	VIF	DWT
Constant	0.002			0.046	0.032		
GEE	0.458	0.421	0.447	3.662	0.004	2.147	
MEE	0.578	0.525	0.574	4.736	0.001	3.098	1.785
AEE	0.541	0.491	0.544	2.150	0.000	2.445	

GEE: Generalized Entrepreneurial Education
MEE: Motivational Entrepreneurial Education
AEE: Augmented Entrepreneurial Education

CHAPTER 5

UNCERTAINTY AND FINANCIAL RISKS FACED BY INTERNATIONAL FINANCIAL INSTITUTIONS

Summary of Chapter Five

The purpose of this chapter is to establish if there is systematic risk, and if it has impact on the profitability, and/or liquidity of the banks in Europe. This chapter uses various financial performance ratios from 100 banks, operating in different European countries, to investigate if such a relationship exists over a five-year period (2011 to 2015). Before working on systematic risk evaluation, we need to know if, in order to shape up the financial structure of any firm, the operating performance has any importance. It is expected that the outcomes of this research are very important from the perspectives of investors and bank managers, as these findings will help them to fully analyze the effects of various strategic choices, keeping in view the risk profiles of banks. Some implications of potential policies which are based on the new capital requirements in view of the risk-leverage relationship have also been discussed in this chapter.

Keywords: Financial Risk, Business Risk, Profitability, Liquidity, systematic risk, financial performance, capital requirements, risk-leverage.

Section 1: Chapter Introduction

Systematic risk has remained a topic of deliberation in economic debates since its emergence in 2007. Now the ongoing financial crisis has become the major topic under discussion in most national and international economic summits and forums, which proves that it is not a new phenomenon anymore. Franklin et al. (2007) stated, while stressing the financial history of Western Europe, that systematic risk is not a new thing. European banks have been experiencing systematic risk in almost every decade within the last 400 years. Systemic risk has its origin inside and outside the financial framework. It can occur from the interconnectedness of specific financial foundations and budgetary markets, and their exposure to the real economy (Szpunar 2012).

The financial crisis has badly affected the global economy. It is considered as the worst crisis since 1930, and it has had a serious impact on the financial markets around the world as well as the global economy as a whole. For this reason, numerous banks inside the Eurozone and America have received bailout packages, keeping in mind the end goal to guarantee congruity of their operations. Nations like Portugal, Ireland, Spain, Italy, and Greece, needed to actualize some monetary arrangements with a specific end goal to draw in bailout support from the European National Bank. A study by Achleitner, Braun, Metzger & Schmidt (2016) stated that technology venture growth and the different prospects of investments were also badly affected due to the financial crisis during this period. They also explained that during the financial crisis, total global financing volume dropped significantly.

As the real objective of the firm is to expand the stockholders' wealth, the researcher will judge the execution on the bases of estimation of the firms. The study's test includes firms records assembled from a hundred European banks. Many firms across the nations reported billions of dollars of loss in the late financial crisis that began in the US and after that, damaged a number of nations. The study period covers 2011 to 2015, when the impacts of the crisis were most pointedly felt by the organizations. The outcomes of the study propose that a European bank's systematic risk is purposely interlinked with the bank's size and imperishable resources, and with the volume of loans in a its financial report. Similarly, we assume that banks with high liquidity and profitability, and also those with high relative levels of advance loss procurement, have a tendency to have lower beta values. The study explained that systematic risk had an influence on the European banks' profitability and liquidity. Contrary to the greater part of the historical literature, our evaluations don't bolster the customary theory that the introduction of deliberate danger adversely corresponds with monetary influence.

The major contribution of the present study is that it contains the wider data set of a hundred European banks. The study period includes data from the banks' 2011 to 2015 annual reports. Another motivation for this study is that its results show newness, and also the uncertainty of risk supervision in the banking industry. It also explains the importance of systematic risk as a safeguard for the solidity of the banking system specifically, and the financial system in general. Systemic risk management requires orientation of supervision to monitor the situation and evolution of national banking systems as a whole, and it is combined with the monetary policies and the micro prudential supervision of banks. The real economies heavily interact with the banking system, which generates repercussions for the banking system, as well as financial stability. This paper contains strong support from previous studies, and also validates evidence based on facts and figures from leading European Banks. The following paper is divided into different sections, so after the introduction, other headings explore the literature review, the research methodology, and empirical analysis, in detail, and finally conclude with recommendations.

Section 2: Critical argument/ Literature Review

a) Systematic risk:

The research examines the main rules of evaluating risk in the European banking sector. The researcher conducted analysis, and explained the evaluation of systematic risk by equity beta. The beta value is also called ‘market risk’ or ‘stock beta’, which is an evaluation of the sensitivity of stocks’ profits to the profits of the financial market overall. Systematic risk and its indicators are examined generally in financial writing, and are viewed as a standout amongst the most intriguing topics in banking studies. The Capital Asset Pricing Model (CAPM) proposes a straight correlation between the beta and the required rate of return of any stock (Sharpe, 1964).

b) Primary accounting determinants of systematic risk in banking sector

There are many determinants of systematic risk which have a major effect on financial economics and institutions. This study examines and verifies the primary accounting determinants of systematic risk in the banking division. The researcher discovered a big data set from the European institutions. In particular, study evaluations were based on market and accounting sector panel information from European banks.

Financial indicators are investigated as ‘could be’ determinants of the systematic risk of banks: Book leverage, liquidity ratio, loan to asset ratio, loan loss ratio, intangibles to assets ratio, and earnings per share, etc. Previous studies have stated many determinants of systematic risk, and many are supported by various researchers. The Capital Asset Pricing Model, created by William Sharp in 1964, constituted a memorable breakthrough in current financial hypothesis, as a principal hypothetical model to acquaint security sensitivity with market risk, which is the systematic risk or beta, as a fundamental determinant of its required rate of return in an all-round broad investment portfolio setting.

a. European banks and US monetary emergencies

The movements in the markers of European banks in 2008 and 2009 show overflow impacts of the financial crisis in the US. Every bank in the market suffered through the loss of Lehman Brothers in 2008. It was noted that in maximum financial crises, systematic risk is shown to be fundamentally determined due to the risk premium component, according to the market impression of the European banks. It is also proposed that the anxiety was for the most part because of increased liquidity storing and risk aversion in the worldwide financial markets.

b. Indicator of liquidity creation and risk

A study by Steffen, Rauch, Tyrrel and Hackethal (2010) covers determinants of liquidity danger, and attempts to perceive the determinants of liquidity creation. Their outcomes highlight that the most pivotal determinants are macroeconomic variables and cash related method, while they do not demonstrate a fundamental relationship between liquidity creation and banks' particular variables, for example, size and execution.

Capital impact on liquidity: Horvàth et al. in a study on Czech banks (2012), demonstrate the capital consequences for bank liquidity creation. The researchers note that, for smaller banks, Basel III may incite banks' diminished liquidity creation by presenting capital requirements more firmly, and is symmetrically more important for liquidity creation which may hamper banks' dissolvability.

Relationship of liquidity, profitability and size: Ahmed, Ahmed and Naqvi, in a study of six Pakistani banks (2011), say that "there is no critical relationship between liquidity danger, productivity and size", while underlining a crucial relationship between liquidity hazard and influence and the measure of banks' generosity.

c. Enhancement of policies through balance of liabilities and assets

The most crucial criteria of instability of any bank dependent upon the spread of a financial crisis are:

1. The number of interbank connections;
2. The volume of interbank exposures;
3. The separation from the rest of the members of the interbank market (measured by the quantity of money-related middlemen, it can be said to be something of a net volume);
4. A systemic significance of counterparties;
5. The position (separation) in an interbank market (system).

d. Main source of risk:

In breaking down the progressions of systemic risk and contagion, starting with one financial organization then passing on to the next, it is key to recognize three essential wellsprings of risk: loan loss banks, the conduct of indebted person banks, and 'middle man' banks, in light of the fact that the probability of default of one bank depends on upon its presentation in another defaulting bank. It is imperative to find an answer to the accompanying inquiry: how the size of the reserves of a loan specialist bank affects the probability of default of a pre-set borrower bank. In a manner of speaking, it is appropriate to make sense of whether the interbank business sector can diminish the effect of the spread of the financial emergency. Also, the higher the bank's presentation in another defaulting bank, the more conspicuous is the probability that investors will rashly pull back their reserves (Furfine 1999). In like manner, the twofold method for the interbank business sector is uncovered: a lender bank can decrease the danger of the financial emergency, or can extend the liquidity risk of an account holder bank.

e. Banks with insolvency issues as a little part of the bank's assets:

Wells (2004) explored the British banking framework based on 2002 information, and exhibited that financial emergency spread decisions are, to some degree, outstanding. Notwithstanding the fact that they have only recovered 4 of the 33 losses of the measure of assets, the bankruptcy of a solitary bank can trigger the various banks. Besides, indebtedness issues can be thought of as just a little part of the banking structure. Be that as it may, the results can be changed a little if the lattice of assets and liabilities of interbank business sector is incorporated with more correct information, i.e. information on the particularly high volume of bank resources held in various banks. The danger of the spread of the financial contagion would then develop; in any case, banks with bankruptcy issues will constitute just a small part of the banking framework resources.

f. Systematic risks additionally constrain advance business sector liquidity

This paper, in like manner, adds to two strands of business sector liquidity literature. As an issue of first significance, it gives a straightforward, yet novel, perspective on how financial specialists can beat potential antagonistic determination and spare business sector liquidity. From the perspective of the possibility of information-based liquidity, the paper is most related to those on the security outline, exhibited by Pennacchi and Gorton (1990), Duffie and Demarzo (1999), and DeMarzo (2005). This flood of composing that hassles business sector liquidity can be made by information on inhumane securities - obligations for instance. Since obligation settlements are steady in all non-bankrupt states, private information on the profits of this hidden resource doesn't prompt unfriendly choice anymore. This paper suggests that, by delivering homogeneous returns, the resources of systematic risk similarly limit the extent of private information and advance business sector liquidity.

g. Influence of systematic risk on profitability and liquidity

Systematic risk has a direct or indirect effect on profitability and liquidity. We can distinguish profitability and liquidity as the final workings of the success of economy achieved by a firm in response to investment in it. Economic success is managed by net profit accounting. The accomplishment of maximum profit depends on the risk accepted by the shareholders; acceptance of more risk increases the chances of more profit, which is the goal of firms operating within economies. These things consider that maximum return is the main component of invested capital in the different projects.

Section 3: Approaches/Methodology

a) Statistical instruments:

In this study, the researcher used data from a hundred European banks to investigate the primary accounting determinants of risk in the banking industry. Three financial pointers are investigated as evaluators of the systematic risk of banks: i) Changes in interest rate; ii) Inflation; and iii) Recession and Wars. According to some past research on systematic risk evaluations, seven variables are usually utilized. This researcher tried to analyze the evaluators of systematic risk. Seven main indicators of systemic risk are used in the current study, which include the volume of intangible resources, the loan portfolio quality, business strength, business operating efficiency, size, degree of diversification, and the cashflow received for each dollar invested in an equity position. To find a symbol wise indicator, the researcher analyzed these given seven indicators across one hundred banks on their five-year data (2011 to 2015). In this methodology, the focus was to check the direct impact of systematic risk on the profitability and liquidity of hundred European banks. For this, the researcher divided the ratios into different parts. For direct impact, the researcher used profitability leverage and liquidity, and for indirect effect, chose size, diversification, volume of intangible resources, cash flow, loan portfolio quality, and business operating efficiency. The present study chose seven systemic risk indictors as independent variables (as mentioned above) and three (earning per share, leverage, and liquidity) as dependent variables.

b) Data

The selected sample of the present study is 100 recorded banks in European nations. The researcher utilized the information of these banks from 2011 – 2015, using helpful sampling. The information used as a part of the current study is accessible on sites and balance-sheet examination through Soft-trax programming. Financial organizations are rejected or excluded from the sample because of various capital structures. The researcher's main focus was to check the systematic risk and define the impact on profitability and liquidity.

Section 4: Empirical analysis

This chapter expresses the value of data which can be checked by using different tools. With a specific end goal to break down accumulated information, the researcher utilized measurable programming, like E-views, which analyzed the results through z-test, t-test, and relapse. The information is exhibited through each and every result as it was generated in E-views, and from other tools.

a) Regression model and equation

Panel information is utilized as a part of current study. This information gives an impact of times arrangement and cross sectional information. For assessing the speculation, the basic effect model has been utilized. The equation is:

EPS = αo + α1ALTL + α2DY + α3EC + α4INTA + α5LLR + α6LTA + α7Size

LEV = αo + α1ALTL + α2DY + α3EC + α4INTA + α5LLR + α6LTA + α7Size

LIQ = αo + α1ALTL + α2DY + α3EC + α4INTA + α5LLR + α6LTA + α7Size

Where an observation shows;

Dependent Variables

LIQ = liquidity
EPS = profitability
LEV = financial leverage

Independent variables:

INTA = volume of intangible resources
LLR = loan portfolio quality
ALTL = business strength
EC = business operating efficiency
SIZE = size
LTA = degree of diversification
DY = cash flow received for each dollar invested in an equity position

The researcher selected one hundred European banks for workings with country details (Appendix, Table1)

Table 1: Data Trend

Variables	Mean	Min	Max	Standard Deviation
ALTL	5.12	0.06	11.60	2.69
DY	0.22	-	3.45	0.51
EC	0.12	(0.72)	0.66	0.18
EPS	0.43	(0.42)	71.31	12.00
INTA	0.21	-	1.05	0.21
LEV	0.11	-	36.27	7.10
LIQ	0.95	0.01	3.33	0.44
LLR	0.36	(0.46)	7.60	1.07
LTA	0.39	0.01	10.72	1.44
Size	5.65	0.39	11.77	1.87

As mentioned in the above table, the values in each variable shows that the trend of data is very clear, and near objects, like the values of mean in same variables, being the same as minimum and maximum values, shows the trend of data values. The standard deviation of each variable shows the total ability in the same variable to access the results. The large variation shows losses in the business and lack of goodwill, or less intangible assets available in the business.

b) Relationship between systematic risk management and bank performance

According to various authors and researchers, systematic risk is the most significant of all risks, related to size of potential losses. As credit expansion is one of the major, and basic, functions of the banking industry, the mitigation of risk (systematic risk) is the centre of banking operations. At the point when banks manage their risk properly, they can reach a favorable position in the market by expanding their performance (return). Good risk management shows that banks manage their operations at lower relative risk, and in fewer conflicting situations (Anthony and Santomero 1997). The advantages of proper risk management lead to better bank policy implementation, and cause increase in banks' return. The banks additionally get more chances to build their productive assets, prompting higher bank profitability, liquidity, and solvency (Tandelilin, Kaaro, Mahadwartha, Supriyatna 2007). In this way, effective systematic risk management is the basic segment of banks' general risk evaluation procedure, and is fundamental to the accomplishment of long-term goals in the banking industry. At the end, the basic thing which banking management should keep in mind is to get sustainable growth and profit, because the ultimate goal of every organization is profit maximization.

c) Discussion of results

The liquidity (LIQ) and profitability (EPS) coefficients are inverse, and measurably significant at 1%, giving proof that higher liquidity and profitability brings down a bank's systematic risk. Driven outcomes from LIQ and EPS are not different because of high performance, and liquid firms are, by and large, seen, *ceteris paribus* (CP), as less unsafe than banks with terrible economic performances or low liquidity levels. This researcher, likewise, settled a solid positive connection, statistically significant at the 1% level, between a bank's equity beta and its loan-to-asset ratio (LTA). The loan to asset proportion is anticipated, in the current research, as an intermediary for bank upgrade levels: the greater the credit portfolio with relative to total assets (LTA), the lower the level of development in non-enthusiasm-creating exercises. Subsequently, our relapse model attests to an inverse relationship among banks' systematic risk and the level of income expansion. This affirmation, regardless of past thought, is dependable with the speculative model on upgrade points of interest, as demonstrated by the way a more elevated amount of expansion declines income and profit instability (since income from exercises in past intermediation are more unfaltering than advance based profit) and furthermore, bankruptcy risk (ensuing premium pay is lower, exaggerated through a potential breakdown in economic credit situations), while developing salary sources and cross-offering opportunities. Positive and significantly important association (1% level of measurable criticalness) is, in like manner, found between systematic risk and bank size, showing that, regardless of the open doors to higher development and the understood open affirmation against frustration, greater banks tend to have higher business area hazard exposure.

Regression analysis:

EPS to independent*:* in the first case, the researcher took earnings per share as dependent variable, and the rest of the seven variables as independent, to check the stability of banks and the ultimate effects on earnings per share (profitability).

Table 3: Earnings per share to independent variables

Dependent Variable: EPS_?				
Method: Pooled Least Squares				
Sample: 2011 to 2015				
Included observations: 5				
Cross-sections included: 100				
Total pool (balanced) observations: 500				
Variable	**Coefficient**	**Std. Error**	**t-Statistic**	**Prob.**
C	**10.14152**	**0.094358**	**107.4789**	**0**
ALTL_?	**0.188371**	**0.011795**	**15.97024**	**0**
DY_?	**0.040738**	**0.006719**	**6.062766**	**0**
EC_?	**-0.802155**	**0.067303**	**-11.91864**	**0**
INTA_?	**-2.682461**	**1.095389**	**-2.448866**	**0.0148**
LLR_?	**0.003076**	**0.001006**	**3.057114**	**0.0024**
LTA_?	**0.003733**	**0.001565**	**2.385507**	**0.0175**
SIZE_?	**-0.001421**	**0.001366**	**-1.039897**	**0.299**

Effects Specification			
Cross-section fixed (dummy variables)			
R-squared	**0.999998**	Mean dependent var	**10.56188**
Adjusted R-squared	**0.999997**	S.D. dependent var	**12.00187**
S.E. of regression	**0.02066**	Akaike info criterion	**-4.734075**
Sum squared resid	**0.167739**	Schwarz criterion	**-3.832149**
Log likelihood	**1290.519**	**Hannan-Quinn criter.**	**-4.380161**
F-statistic	**1588728**	**Durbin-Watson stat**	**2.141443**

The results in Table 3 show that there are direct relationships between earnings and size, and other factors. The value of p is not significant with variable 'size' relationship with 'earnings per share'. This shows that all variables have significant impact on earnings per share (profitability) except 'size' of European banks. The adjusted R square value explained that one unit change in systematic risk indicator caused 99% change in all earnings per share. Durbin Watson shows that there is no issue of multi-colinarity in the results, and F statistics show that the overall model is significant in nature.

Leverage to independent variables: The second case is taking leverage as dependent variable and the rest of the seven variables as independent variables to check the strength and leverage ratio of the banks and the ultimate effects on banks' performance.

The results in Table 4 show that there are direct relationships between leverage and other factors. As in relationship analysis, the table shows that all variable P-Values are less than 0.05, and it is stated that a relationship exists between all systematic risk determinants and the leverage ratio of the bank. The adjusted R square value explains that one unit change in systematic risk indicator caused 88% change in all earnings per share. Durbin Watson shows that there is no issue of multi-colinarity in the results and F statistics show that the overall model is significant in nature.

Table 4: Leverage to independent variables

Dependent Variable: LEV?				
Method: Pooled Least Squares				
Sample: 2011 2015				
Included observations: 5				
Cross-sections included: 100				
Total pool (balanced) observations: 500				
Variable	**Coefficient**	**Std. Error**	**t-Statistic**	**Prob.**
C	**-13.60591**	**10.83522**	**-1.255711**	**0.21**
ALTL_?	**2.746399**	**1.354444**	**2.027695**	**0.0433**
DY_?	**0.600275**	**0.77159**	**0.777972**	**0.0371**
EC_?	**6.212146**	**7.728401**	**0.803807**	**0.0422**
INTA_?	**-23.95149**	**125.7843**	**-0.190417**	**0.0449**
LLR_?	**0.007099**	**0.115538**	**0.061447**	**0.051**
LTA_?	**1.745124**	**0.179715**	**9.710534**	**0.000**
SIZE_?	**1.668171**	**0.156865**	**10.63445**	**0.000**
Effects Specialization				
Cross-section fixed (dummy variables)				

R-squared	**0.912045**	Mean dependent var	**10.16746**
Adjusted R-squared	**0.888322**	S.D. dependent var	**7.098974**
S.E. of regression	**2.372352**	Akaike info criterion	**4.752842**
Sum squared resid	**2211.825**	Schwarz criterion	**5.654768**
Log likelihood	**-1081.211**	**Hannan-Quinn criter.**	**5.106756**
F-statistic	**38.44538**	**Durbin-Watson stat**	**1.561555**

Liquidity to independent variables: In the third case, the researcher took liquidity as the dependent variable and the rest of the seven variables as independent variables to check the strength and liquidity of the banks and the ultimate effects on banks' performance.

Table 5: Liquidity to independent variables

Dependent Variable: LIQ_?				
Method: Pooled Least Squares				
Sample: 2011 2015				
Included observations: 5				
Cross-sections included: 100				
Total pool (balanced) observations: 500				
Variable	**Coefficient**	**Std. Error**	**t-Statistic**	**Prob.**
C	**0.576062**	**0.117615**	**4.897875**	**0**
ALTL_?	**0.235892**	**0.014702**	**16.04458**	**0**
DY_?	**0.04403**	**0.008375**	**5.257029**	**0**
EC_?	**-0.122085**	**0.083891**	**-1.455292**	**0.1464**
INTA_?	**-1.35015**	**1.36537**	**-0.988853**	**0.3233**
LLR_?	**0.001821**	**0.001254**	**1.452231**	**0.1472**
LTA_?	**0.008339**	**0.001951**	**4.274544**	**0**
SIZE_?	**0.015884**	**0.001703**	**9.328727**	**0**
Effects Specification				
Cross-section fixed (dummy variables)				
R-squared	**0.997323**	Mean dependent var	**1.50534**	
Adjusted R-squared	**0.996601**	S.D. dependent var	**0.441681**	
S.E. of regression	**0.025752**	Akaike info criterion	**-4.293444**	
Sum squared resid	**0.260615**	Schwarz criterion	**-3.391518**	
Log likelihood	**1180.361**	**Hannan-Quinn criter.**	**-3.939529**	

The results of Table 5 show that there are dircct relationships between leverage and size, and other factors, which means the bank's liquidity closes with performance of size and its impact of liquidity for loans. The adjusted R square value explained that one unit change in systematic risk indicator caused 99% change in all earnings per share. Durbin Watson shows that there is no issue of multi-colinarity in the results, and F statistics show that the overall model is significant in nature.

Section 5: Conclusion and discussion

a) Regression estimator discussion

Running an arrangement of determination tests, a relapse estimator including both bank and year settled impacts was picked as our reference model. Confirmation from this model demonstrates that bank equity beta is essentially and firmly associated with bank size (book estimation of total assets) and with the relative volume of advances and intangibles in bank total assets (loan to asset proportion and intangibles to asset proportion, separately). Also, we note that bank systematic risk is basically and antagonistically related with a bank's benefit, as measured by income per offer, liquidity levels, i.e. the cash to assets proportion, and loan loss proportion, that is, the extent of arrangement for loan losses to gross advances. As inspected, some of these revelations, specifically the effects of intangibles and loan loss arrangements on banks systematic risk, in a roundabout way plot the part of financial exposure and shrewd accounting conduct in defining the stock market system discernments around a bank's systematic risk. In the meantime, the positive relationship between the loan to asset proportion and systematic risk, in a roundabout way, affirms diversification advantages. It is likewise remarkable that there is a leverage hazard relationship in the Italian banking structure. Without a doubt, we discover no factually powerful verification for the standard theory that less-leveraged banks are seen by speculators as less hazardous. This discovery construes the - for the most part - little importance of capital adequacy as an intermediary for banks' unwavering quality.

b) European countries insider reviews

Spain and Italy are the two countries with the highest amount of total shortage, 2.235 million and 2.101 million respectively, whereas European Russia and Germany have no shortage. This highlight emphasizes the Spanish and Italian distress during 2011, even if these sums were below those at the end of 2009. Germany's results show that its banks are well capitalized and no capital injection is required. European and Russian banks were already recapitalized at this date which explains the 0 value. This table also shows that the domestic impact of these banks evolves over time, which is a good property. Indeed, the Greek shortage reached its peak of 2.811 million Euros in this table on December 31, 2009, during the sovereign debt crisis, and declined to 349 million Euros on December 30, 2011. This result captures the bailout of the Greek economy, which started in 2010.

c) Mitigating systematic risk

Perceiving the issue of systematic risk, financial firms coordinated the dangers associated with the disappointments of other monetary firms to point of limit quite a while ago. A case in point, before the production of the Federal Reserve System in 1913, business banks concocted clearing house game plans attempting to shield themselves from managing account alarms. The fundamental part of a clearing house is to clear checks and diverse sorts of instalments between partner banks. In the 19th century, clearing houses made frameworks to shield their people from banking solidity, and to give additional liquidity to banks going up against runs on their reserves. For example, clearing house individuals could motivate authentications to settle their parities with other partner banks in lieu of cash or distinctive reserves. Further, clearing houses in general guarantee the instalment commitments of people incapacitated by reserve withdrawals. For instance, financial sector trades for the Chicago Mercantile Exchange, are moreover private game plans that limit systematic risks.

d) Recommendations

There is likewise, a requirement for banks to adopt sound corporate governance practices, deal with their risks in an incorporated methodology or integrated approach, concentrate on core banking activities, and hold fast to prudential banking practices. Finally, the debt structure of financial institutions could be explored all the more nearly, since it is regularly the level of short-term debt which is pivotal while deciding the robustness of financial institutions. The methodology in this paper does not differentiate between short-term and long-term debt, hence it neglects to catch the impact that the debt structure may have on the robustness of financial institutions.

References

Achleitner A, K., Braun, R., Metzger, G and Schmidt, M. 2016. The impact of the financial crisis on financing technology ventures, *Int. J. of Entrepreneurship and Small Business,*29(1), 4 – 24, DOI: 10.1504/IJESB.2016.078051

Ahmed, N., Ahmed, Z., and Naqvi, I. 2011. Liquidity risk and Islamic Banks: Evidence from Pakistan. Interdisciplinary, *Journal of Research in Business*, 1(9), 99-102.

Anthony M. Santomero, 1997. Commercial Bank Risk Management: an Analysis of the Process, *The Warton School University of Pennsylvania*

DeMarzo, P., 2005. The Pooling and Tranching of Securities: A Model of Informed Intermediation, *Review of Financial Studies*, 18, 1-35.

DeMarzo, P, and Duffie, D, 1999. A Liquidity-Based Model of Security Design, *Econometrica*, 67, 65-99.

Dang, Jha, P., Koshy, A., & Sharma, D. 2005. An Empirical Analysis of Different Types of Consumers Promotions in India Market. *Asian Journal of Marketing*, 104-122.

Franklin A, & Gale, D., 2007. Understanding Financial Crises, *Oxford University Press Inc*; 1-4. available at: Århus School of Business Library.

Furfine, C.H. 1999. The microstructure of the federal funds market. *Financial Markets, Institutions, and Instruments* 8, no. 5:24–44.

Gorton, G., & Pennacchi, G. 1990. Financial Intermediaries and Liquidity Creation, *The Journal of Finance*, 45, 49-71

Horvat, R., Seidler, J. and Weill, L. 2012. Bank's capital and liquidity creation: Granger causality evidence. *Working Paper Series 5, Czech National Bank.*

Rauch, C., Steffen, S., Hackethal, A., Tyrell, M., 2010. Determinants of Bank Liquidity Creation, Available at: http://papers.ssrn.com/sol3/papers.cfm?abstract_id=1343595.

Szpunar, P. J. and Głogowski, A. 2012. Lending in foreign currencies as a systemic risk. *Macro-prudential Commentaries,* 4, ESRB, 5.

Sharpe, W. F. 1964. Capital Asset Prices: A Theory of Market Equilibrium Under Conditions of Risk, *The Journal of Finance* 19(3), 425-442

Tandelilin, E., Kaaro, H., Mahadwartha, P. A. and Supriyatna, S. 2007. Corporate Governance, Risk Management and Bank Performance: Does Type of Ownership Matter? *EADN Working Paper*, 34.

Appendix

Table 2: 100 European banks with country details

Sr. No	Bank Name	Country Name
1	Credit Europe Bank NV	UK
2	Deutsche Post Bank	UK
3	DNB ASA	Norway
4	First Investment Bank AD	UK
5	GENIKI Bank of Greece SA	Greece
6	GrønlandsBANKEN AS	European Russia
7	GSD Holding AS	Norway
8	HYPO NOE Gruppe Bank AG	UK
9	Hypothekenbank Frankfurt AG	UK
10	Iccrea Holding SpA	Norway
11	CaisseRégionalede CréditAgricoleMutuelAtlantiqueVendée	European Russia
12	Compagnie de FinancementFoncier	France
13	Crédit du Nord SA	Romanian
14	Nationwide Building Society	UK
15	Nordea Bank AB	Sweden
16	Nordea Bank Norge ASA	Sweden, Northern Europe
17	Nordea Bank Polska SA	Greece
18	Nordjyske Bank AS	European Russia
19	NORDLB NorddeutscheLandesbankGirozentrale	European Russia
20	Nova Ljubljanska Banka d.d	European Russia
21	OAO MDM Bank	European Russia
22	OAO VTB Bank	European Russia
23	OldenburgischeLandesbank AG	UK
24	PJSC Bank Saint-Petersburg	European Russia
25	Lollands Bank AS	Denmark
26	MelhusSparebank	Norway
27	MünchenerHypothekenbankEg	Norway
28	National Bank of Greece SA	Denmark
29	Nordfyns Bank AS	Denmark
30	Nørresundby Bank AS	Denmark
31	OAO Absolut Bank	European Russia
32	ÖsterreichischeVolksbanken-AG	UK
33	Østjydsk Bank AS	Denmark
34	Rabobank Group	European Netherlands

35	RaiffeisenZentralbankÖsterreich AG	UK
36	RaiffeisenlandesbankOberösterreich AG	UK
37	Russian Agricultural Bank	European Russia
38	Tekstilbank AS	Denmark
39	Van Lanschot NV	European Netherlands
40	VP Bank AG	UK
41	WestdeutscheGenossenschafts-Zentralbank AG	UK
42	AlbarakaTürkKatilimBankasi AS	Denmark
43	AO Raiffeisenbank	European Netherlands
44	Arion bankihf	European Netherlands
45	AsyaKatilimBankasi AS	Denmark
46	AT Rodovid Bank	Ukraine
47	Attica Bank SA	Greece
48	AurskogSparebank	Norway
49	Banca Popolare di Bergamo SpA	Italy
50	Banco di Desio e della Brianza SpA	Italy
51	Bank für Tirol und Vorarlberg AG	UK
52	Bank of Cyprus Public Company Limited	Cyprus
53	Bankinter SA	Greece
54	BN Bank ASA	Greece
55	Bristol & West Plc	UK
56	Cacanskabankaa.d.Cacak	UK
57	CaisseRégionale de CréditAgricoleMutuel de Nord de France	European Russia
58	Central Cooperative Bank AD	UK
59	Clydesdale Bank Plc	UK
60	CréditAgricole Corporate and Investment Bank	European Russia
61	ABH Financial Limited	Turkey
62	Banca ComercialaCarpatica SA	Romanian
63	Banca Transilvania SA	Romanian
64	Banco Bilbao Vizcaya Argentaria, SA	Romanian
65	Bank BPH SA	Romanian
66	Bank for Development and Foreign Economic Affairs (Vnesheconombank)	European Russia
67	Banque et Caissed'Epargne de l'Etat, Luxembourg	Romanian
68	BGL BNP Paribas SA	Romanian
69	BHW Bausparkasse AG	UK
70	BNP Paribas Fortis SA	Romanian
71	IKB Deutsche Industriebank AG	UK
72	Íslandsbankihf	European Russia
73	JSC UniCredit Bank	European Russia

74	Komercijalna Banka a.d. Beograd	Serbia
75	Kreditbanken AS	Denmark
76	Landshypotek Bank AB (publ)	Sweden
77	MünchenerHypothekenbankeG	Germany
78	Crédit Lyonnais SA	Romanian
79	CréditMutuelArkéa	Romanian
80	Deka Bank Group	Germany
81	DEPFA BANK Plc	Germany
82	Deutsche Hypothekenbank AG	UK
83	Deutsche Kreditbank AG	UK
84	Deutsche Zentral-Genossenschaftsbank AG	UK
85	EurobankErgasias SA	Romanian
86	GENIKI Bank of Greece SA	Romanian
87	Iccrea Banca SpA	France
88	Crédit Lyonnais SA	Romanian
89	ProCredit Holding AG & Co. KGaA	UK
90	Santander Consumer Finance, SA	Greece
91	SEB Pank AS	Latvia
92	Šiaulių bankas AB	Sweden
93	SkandinaviskaEnskildaBanken AB	Sweden
94	SpareBanken Vest	Norway
95	SvenskaHandelsbanken AB	Singapore
96	Swedbank AB	Sweden
97	TürkiyeVakiflarBankasi TAO	Turkey
98	UniCredit Bank Czech Republic and Slovakia, a.s	Central and Eastern Europe
99	VorarlbergerLandes-und Hypothekenbank AG	UK
100	West Bromwich Building Society	UK

CHAPTER 6

GLOBAL CHALLENGES THROUGH ENTERPRISE RISK MANAGEMENT SOLUTIONS

Summary of Chapter Six

The aim of this chapter is to find the impact of Enterprise Risk Management (ERM) implementation on the financial performance of the world's Takaful industry. In this regard, the ERM implementation level has been measured. Two control variables, age and gross domestic product (GDP) are also employed. On the other side, financial performance is measured in terms of its indicators; return on investments (ROI) and earnings per share (EPS). A sample of 30 Takaful firms from 10 countries has been taken over a period of four years (2012-2015). This chapter uses quantitative measures and secondary data for this purpose. The hypotheses are being tested, one by one, through correlation and regression analysis. The findings can be utilized for the advancement of ERM within the Takaful industry, making it a strong industry rather than a business risk.

Keywords: Enterprise Risk Management (ERM), Financial Performance (FP), Return on Investment, Earning per Share, Chief Risk Officer, Firm size, age, Gross Domestic Product, Regression, Takaful industry

Section 1: Chapter introduction

Enterprise risk management is an invention of this century, and it has emerged mainly as an approach which addresses the limitations of traditional risk management. It's a key subject, especially for those firms which desire success in the future. Since its commencement, it has become a standard instrument to manage the diversified risks of organization, dealing with operational as well as strategic risks, and transfiguring the risks into opportunities. The main goal behind the advent of ERM is the well-coordinated management of all the risks of an organization, ranging from corporate governance, auditing, information technology, and distribution systems, to human resources. The arrival of ERM is not an obsession, but a natural evolution of risk management, so that risks can be managed at organization wide level (Fraser et al. 2011).

In the ERM approach, all risks are identified and the corresponding risk responses are taken according to the defined risk appetite of an organization. When it comes to Islamic finance, the concept of risk management is an important part of the ultimate goal of society's well-being, both social and economic. Takaful is a tool which is used in Islamic finance to perform the function of risk management by protecting people and their property. In Shariah, the main function of Takaful is to lessen worries and uncertainties, provide contingency damages, and shield the owner and his belongings.

This study discusses the ERM implementation level of the Takaful industry, which has been considered ineffective, and has turned into a big risk. The implementation of ERM is not that fluent, because many of its areas are still untouched and require exploration for a better understanding and smooth implementation. So, those firms that are already implementing it are also facing difficulties in spite of the availability of all main resources. The lack of work is one of the main impediments which make ERM implementation more difficult to perform, because there is a dearth of success stories. Evidence has been found that among the various potential risks for the global Takaful industry, ineffective ERM has been at the top, although this has been addressed slightly, bringing it from no. 3 to no. 5 in the top business risks list of the global Takaful industry. So, this research will actually focus on the ERM implementation level of the Takaful industry, and will analyze its proposed impact on financial performance.

The aim of the study is to analyze the relationship between ERM implementation levels and return on investments and earnings per share of the world's Takaful firms. This paper is divided into four headings. The second section will provide the literature review which covers the theoretical and empirical literature of the Islamic Takaful industry, performance measures, enterprise risk management (ERM) and its variables, explanation and links between these variables, and ROI and EPS. The third section demonstrates the research methodology of the paper. The fourth section will present analysis and empirical findings, and the fifth section finally concludes the overall study.

Section 2: Critical review

For a long time, organizations have been managing their risks through transferring them to the insurance firms, or through planning. But in this world of globalization and the start of a new century, firms were exposed to enormous and diversified risks - natural and man-made - which eventually affected the firm's strategic ability to achieve their goals, both, short and long term. This situation moved the risk management phenomenon to the executive table, and called it a responsibility of senior management. This trend of diversified risks gave birth to the consolidated concept of enterprise risk management (Togok et al. 2014).

a) Enterprise Risk Management

The use of new risk management functions ultimately increased the time and cost investment. All these encounters have moved organizations in the direction of managing risk in a completely new, holistic way. This gave birth to the new concept of risk management called ERM, which discourages the silo-based approach and enforces the management of all types of risk in the form of a portfolio.

Different visions exist regarding ERM in the circle of regulatory bodies. Some associate it directly with organizational objectives (COSO 2004, IIA 2009). On the opposite side, some consider risks independent of organizational goals, and argue that there is no link between them. Another aspect causing conflict is the way risk is seen. One school of thought considers risk as an opportunity to excel (CAS 2003) whereas others see risk as a large problem that should be eradicated promptly (RIMS 2007).

b) ERM concept justification

i. Risk and Insurance Management Society (RIMS):

The Risk and Insurance Management Society (RIMS), is an international, nonprofit organization. According to RIMS, enterprise risk management (ERM) is a strategic business discipline that supports the achievement of an organization's objectives by addressing the full spectrum of its risks and managing the combined impact of those risks as an interrelated risk portfolio.

ii. RIMS' risk maturity model (RMM)

RMM is made up of certain important indicators and activities that contribute to the development of a more robust ERM program, which can be maintained and repeated in the long course. The ERM program's self-assessment against the risk indicators identifies the strength of the organizational risk management efforts. At the end, it assigns each organization's ERM program with a maturity score, which ranges from level 1 (lowest risk maturity level) to level 5 (advanced risk maturity level) (RIMS 2007).

iii. The Institute of Internal Auditors (IIA)

The IIA has defined ERM in the following way: Enterprise-wide risk management (ERM) is a structured, consistent and continuous process across the whole organization for identifying, assessing, deciding on responses to, and reporting on, opportunities and threats that affect the achievement of its objectives (IIA 2009). This paper explains the roles of internal auditors by suggesting what internal auditors should and shouldn't do in following the ERM process. They have divided the 18 activities of the ERM process into three main divisions:

1. Core internal audit roles in regard to ERM
2. Legitimate internal audit roles with safeguards
3. Roles which internal audit should not undertake

iv. Standards & Poor (S&P) ratings:

In 2005, Standards & Poor (S&P) introduced ERM for financial institutions in its rating criteria. The motive of this introduction was to consider the risk management and strategy characteristics of an organization in the rating criteria, and for this purpose a portion of the rating criteria was fixed for ERM evaluation (Standard & Poor 2005). The ratings of S&P were developed in the form of an index which has the ultimate goal of evaluating the risk management systems, processes, culture and practices within a firm.

c) Emergence of ERM

According to the results of a survey, which was developed and conducted with the help of experts from the Strategic Risk Management Council conference board, there are main five drivers behind the implementation of ERM (Gates 2006). These comprise: meeting corporate governance requirements (66%), strategic management of risks (60%), regulatory compliance (53%), board demand (51%) and achievement of certain competitive advantage (41%). Here is a list of the main forces, derived from the literature.

Risk Complexity: The foremost force behind ERM is the variety of today's risks. The global mode of business, terrorist activities, and economic conditions around the globe are the producers of these risks. Besides these numerous risks, organizations are also affected by the mutual interaction of these risks. Consequently, it's not irrational to expect another unique lot of risks in the near future. So, organizations have become aware of the necessity and significance of managing all risks collectively, in terms of their size and ability to be measured quantitatively (CAS 2003).

Exterior Pressure: The expectation of companies to increase their ratings is also influencing them to pursue the ERM. As the world's top rating agencies, such as Standard & Poor, Moody, and Fitch, are taking into account ERM implementation while evaluating organizational operations, so ERM implementation has a strong impact upon ratings that are ultimately being issued (Gates 2006).

Corporate Failures and Regulatory Requirements: Although firms decide to adopt ERM for other promising benefits, compliance with the regulatory authorities has really compelled ERM implementation (Pagach & Warr 2010). Some famous compliance requirements around the globe include the Sarbanes-Oxley Act (SOX) in the US, the UK's Corporate Governance Code, the CoCo Report in Canada, Basel II, and the New York Stock Exchange Corporate Governance Rules (Zhao et al. 2014).

d) Enterprise risk management implementation level

In the literature, the following indicators have been associated with the adoption and implementation of ERM in any organization:

Chief Risk Officer: The Chief Risk Officer is a new-fangled position, coined and incorporated at the start of this century. Before that, a corporate risk manager occupied a low level position in the organizational structure, whose key responsibility was to purchase insurance. However, with the increased importance and complexity of risk management, a senior executive position called Chief Risk Officer (CRO) has been incorporated within organizations to identify and measure all types of risk (Nocco & Stulz 2006).

Audit Committee: Paape & Speklé (2012) concluded that the existence of an audit committee in an organization contributes towards its ERM implementation.

Risk Management Committee: The participation of different managerial levels in the implementation of ERM really does matter. A strong association has been found between the formation of a risk management committee and providing proper ERM training to senior executives with ERM maturity (Beasley et al. 2015).

Board Size: A push from the regulatory authorities has really impelled organizations to strengthen their risk management processes and question the role of the Board of Directors in risk oversight. Boards of Directors need detailed knowledge on their organizational operations to make strategic decisions. The relationship between the large number of Board members and the additional organizational value has been seen in literature (Lynall et al. 2003).

Board independence: Board independence is the percentage of the board of directors, who are independent. There is substantial evidence available about the impact of board support to implement the ERM. It has been reported by Beasley et al. (2005) that firms with a higher board independence percentage are further on the way towards the ERM implementation, which means the greater the proportion of independent board members, the higher the stage of ERM implementation is.

S&P's ERM Rating: After the issuance of S&P's ERM ratings, it has become important to evaluate the risk management process of a firm. Initially, this was focused on insurance firms, but more recently, other, non-financial, firms also have been included (McShane et al. 2011).

Big Four Audit Firms (FBA): The literature of auditing has enforced that those firms associated with 'big four' audit companies deliver higher quality audits. Such firms are expected to implement ERM, because these larger auditing firms influence and inspire their customers to improve their risk management practices.

Firm Size: ERM implementation is also likely to be affected by the size of the firm. ERM is costly to implement fully, and customarily, large organizations are more formal; that's why they are more inclined towards ERM recognition than smaller firms (Paape & Speklé 2012).

International Diversification: The relationship between international diversification and the resultant value of the firm has been mixed. There are many studies which suggested a strong relation between them (Denis et al. 2002) but many contrary results are also on the list.

Institutional Ownership: Shareholders have a keen interest in ERM implementation, as they are the final beneficiaries of the enhanced value creation and better decisions regarding different risks. However, the effectiveness of stockholder pressure is dependent upon whether the firm is under institutional ownership, or is an owner-managed firm. A strong correlation has been found between the implementation of ERM and listing on the European Stock Exchange (Paape & Speklé 2012).

Growth: ERM has greater value for those firms which are going through substantial growth than for others, as this growth momentum requires the firm to develop a comprehensive risk management system to tackle all the emerging uncertainties.

e) ERM implementation level and the financial performance of a firm

The relationship between risk and value has been the topic of investigation in research for a long time. The main purpose of inculcating the different risk management systems in an organization is to lessen risks and increase the firm's value (Woods 2009). The different risk management programs cause improvement in the performance of a firm because they save it from different type of loss, such as bankruptcy and reputational damage (Gordon et al. 2009). The external pressures of compliance with regulatory authorities have really damaged the role of ERM as a decision-making tool in organizations. The differences in terms of its measurement techniques, and ambiguity in defining its role, have restricted the utilization of ERM, so that implementation has been turned into a task of mere compliance with the regulators, conflicting with its central purpose of risk mitigation and improved firm performance, and ultimately having no effect on them (Arena et al. 2011).

f) Hypothesis development

H1a: There is a positive relationship between the appointment of a Chief Risk Officer and return on investment in the Takaful industry.

H1b: There is a positive relationship between the appointment of a Chief Risk Officer and earnings per share of the Takaful industry.

H2a: There is a positive relationship between the establishment of a Risk Management Committee and return on investment in the Takaful industry.

H2b: There is a positive relationship between the establishment of a Risk Management Committee and earnings per share of the Takaful industry.

H3a: There is a positive relationship between Board independence and return on investments in the Takaful industry.

H3b: There is a positive relationship between Board independence and earnings per share of the Takaful industry.

H4a: There is a positive relationship between the appointment of a 'big four' audit firm and return on investments in the Takaful industry.

H4b: There is a positive relationship between the appointment of a 'big four' audit firm and earnings per share of the Takaful industry.

H5a: There is a positive relationship between firm size and return on investment in the Takaful industry.

H5b: There is a positive relationship between firm size and earnings per share of the Takaful industry.

H6a: There is a positive relationship between international diversification and return on investments in the Takaful industry.

H6b: There is a positive relationship between international diversification and earnings per Share of the Takaful industry.

H7a: There is a positive relationship between institutional ownership and return on investment in the Takaful industry.

H7b: There is a positive relationship between institutional ownership and earnings per share of the Takaful industry.

H8a: There is a positive relationship between revenue growth and return on investment in the Takaful industry.

H8b: There is a positive relationship between revenue growth and earnings per share of the Takaful industry.

Section 3: Approaches/Methodology

Statistical tool: The current study has panel data, which is also known as cross-sectional time series data; because in panel data, all cases have been observed over two or more periods of time. The main data source of this study is secondary in nature. After the collection of secondary data from the official financial statements of Takaful firms, the data was analyzed in EViews8, Econometric Views software. The research under investigation is basically a quantitative study which is descriptive in nature. Descriptive analysis was performed to describe the general nature of the data. Pearson's correlation was calculated to describe the correlation coefficients of all variables with each other, using a correlation matrix. Regression was performed through the Generalized Method of Moments (GMM).

Data: In the current study, the area of interest which has been taken to investigate is the world's Takaful industry. There are a total of 103 Takaful firms in the world (Al Huda 2016). So the population of the study is the world's Takaful industry. 30 firms were selected by employing four years of their financial statements (2012-2015), inclusive. Takaful firms from 10 countries, including Saudi Arabia, Malaysia, Bahrain, Bangladesh, Kuwait, Qatar, UAE, Oman, Sri Lanka, and Pakistan, were chosen for analysis. This selection was made on the basis of availability, and all those firms have been selected from the industry, which maintains annual financial statements on a regular basis.

Section 4: Data analysis

There are many famous measures of dispersions, but to discuss the sample data of this study, only mean, standard deviation, minimum and maximum values are being taken into consideration.

Descriptive analysis results

Variables	**Mean**	**Maximum**	**Minimum**	**Std. Dev.**
ROI	6.778858	165.6752	-163.792	31.6956
EPS	0.166003	1.912314	-0.77245	0.407309
CRO	0.125	1	0	0.332106
BI	27.528	100	0	27.17825
RMC	0.433333	1	0	0.497613
FS	8.126519	10.14925	6.70647	0.797169
ID	0.066667	1	0	0.25049
IO	7.212157	84.92	0	20.36931
FBA	0.8	1	0	0.401677
RG	123.5032	13231.37	-432.377	1208.046
GDP	4.730833	9.3	0.5	1.443373
AGE	11.23333	36	0	8.633269

In the third dimension of financial performance, ROI comes with mean of 6.79, standard deviation of 31.6956. This means that although the average is good, the data consists of values which are too big at one end and too small on the other. This dispersion in data can be due to the choice of countries, which are very different in terms of their economies, ultimately affecting the financial performance of different institutions. Last, but not least, the financial performance indicator under discussion in the following study is the EPS. It has a mean of 0.166003 with standard deviation of 0.407309. On average, it also appears with a positive mean for the Takaful firms. CRO has a standard deviation of 0.332106, which implies that the deviation of the values from the mean is normally spread. The average 27.528 of the BI shows that the majority of the firms are still in low board independence situations, but the dispersion of the data is wide, which states that there are differentiated situations in terms of board independence. FS has a strong average of 8.126519 which is quite good, and indicates that lion's share of the industry is being segmented on the basis of firm size. The mean of ID is 0.066667, which is very low, and near to zero. This suggests that a tiny number of the Takaful firms are internationally diversified. IO has resulted in an average value of 7.212157, which is good enough, and shows that on average, there is a very low ratio of firms which are under institutional ownership. The average FBA is 0.8, which is definitely a vigorous indicator, and obviously shows that the majority of the firms are being externally audited by one of the 'big four' auditing firms. RG has been identified with a mean of 123.5032 which is not that good when it's being analyzed. It is obvious that the firms' revenue growth is not remarkable as an industry, and there is big deviation from the mean value.

Regression analysis of ROI and EPS

Variable	Prob (ROI)	Prob (EPS)
C	0.0000	0.0000
CRO	0.0000	0.0040
RMC	0.0943	0.4304
BI	0.2212	0.0205
FBA	0.0000	0.9922
FS	0.0000	0.0000
ID	0.3251	0.0107
IO	0.0278	0.5158
RG	0.0066	0.8817
AGE	0.4930	0.0000
GDP	0.0000	0.0303
R-squared	0.501962	0.244748
Adjusted R-squared	0.400321	0.090614
Durbin-Watson stat	2.360215	2.179132
J-statistic	0.019181	0.907459
Prob (J-statistic)	0.889848	0.340790

Return on investment: The results have proved that the fitness of the model is good, as R-squared has a value of 0.501962. Another important indicator is the value of the Durbin Watson test. It actually shows that there is no issue of auto-correlation as it has a value of 2.360215, which is near to 2 (no auto-correlation). In addition, the p-value of the J statistic is 0.889848, which is greater than 0.05, the ultimate proof of the validity of the instrument that has been institutionalized to remove issues of endogeneity. The dimensions of the independent variable, CRO, FBA, FS, IO, RG and GDP, are significant at 5%. There is just a single dimension of ERM implementation which is significant at 10%, and that is RMC.

Earnings per share: The results have proved that the fitness of the model is good, as R-squared has a value of 0.244748. The Durbin Watson test actually shows that there is no issue of auto-correlation. The four dimensions of ERM implementation have proved a significant regression towards earnings per share of Takaful firms. These dimensions are Chief Risk Officer, Board independence, firm size and international diversification.

Section 5: Chapter conclusion

Enterprise Risk Management is a concept of this new era, an approach towards efficient and effective risk management by managing the interconnection of all business risks in one place, in the form of a portfolio. This discourages the management of risks in a traditional way, by isolating them, which ultimately doesn't address the interactions of the variables, proving it to be an inefficient method of risk management. On the basis of all the statistical analysis, the results are found in favor of the relationship. The majority of the dimensions to measure the ERM implementation level which have been included in the study are affecting the financial performance. Many of the results are in line with the previous literature, and claim that the ERM implementation level has a positive impact on the financial performance of the Takaful industry. The financial performance in terms of EPS is also found to be positively associated with ERM implementation, as has been observed in literature (Laisasikorn & Rompho 2014). Hence, it's time to convert the element of ineffective ERM within the Takaful industry into a tool. This tool will definitely help lift the financial performance of the industry, in both accounting and market terms. By managing diverse risks into a portfolio, a unique source of competitive advantage would be generated in the Takaful industry.

Recommendations:

- There is a strong need to manage the risks of Takaful firms in a holistic way by integrating ERM. As Takaful is also being used to meet the risks of the ordinary, as well as business, life, it's of utmost importance that Takaful operators handle their own risks.

- The study is performed in different countries, and suggests that the risk culture is also an important factor which differentiates firms in their level of ERM implementation. ERM is teamwork that needs to be spread over all organizational levels to make its implementation smoother and its results more fruitful.
- There is a great need to develop a unified ERM framework for the industry, which targets the all industry-specific needs of the Takaful industry. This introduction will ultimately cause an increase in the adoption of ERM within the industry. In the longer run, this type of implementation will smooth the process of implementation, approaching it with robust results.

Limitations of the research

Every research has some limitations, and so does the current study. Every effort has been made to make it more effective and authentic. These are the limitations of the current study:

- The study was performed through the single source of data which is secondary data, because of limited resources.
- There was a limitation regarding the non-availability of data. The official websites were not being managed for historical data.

References

Arena, M., Arnaboldi, M., & Azzone, G. (2011). *Is enterprise risk management real?. www.tandfonline.com*, [online] http://www.tandfonline.com/doi/abs/10.1080/13669877.2011.571775

Beasley, M., Branson, B., & Pagach, D. (2015). An analysis of the maturity and strategic impact of investments in ERM. *Journal Of Accounting And Public Policy*, *34*(3), 219-243. [Online] http://dx.doi.org/10.1016/j.jaccpubpol.2015.01.001

Beasley, M., Clune, R., & Hermanson, D. (2005). Enterprise risk management: An empirical analysis of factors associated with the extent of implementation. *Journal Of Accounting And Public Policy*, *24*(6), 521-531.

CAS, (2003). *Overview of Enterprise Risk Management. www.casact.org.* [online] https://www.casact.org/area/erm/overview.pdf

COSO, (2004). *Enterprise Risk Management — Integrated Framework - Executive Summary*. *www.coso.org*. [online] http://www.coso.org/documents/COSO_ERM_ExecutiveSummary.pdf

Denis, D., Denis, D., & Yost, K. (2002). Global Diversification, Industrial Diversification, and Firm Value. *The Journal Of Finance*, *57*(5), 1951-1979. [online] http://dx.doi.org/10.1111/0022-1082.00485

Fraser, J., Schoening-Thiessen, K., & Simkins, B. (2011). Who Reads What Most Often?: A Survey of Enterprise Risk Management Literature Read by Risk Executives. *Enterprise Risk Management*, 385-417. [online] http://dx.doi.org/10.1002/9781118267080.ch22

Gates, S. (2006). Incorporating Strategic Risk into Enterprise Risk Management: A Survey of Current Corporate Practice. *Journal Of Applied Corporate Finance*, *18*(4), 81-90.

Gordon, L., Loeb, M., & Tseng, C. (2009). Enterprise risk management and firm performance: A contingency perspective. *Journal Of Accounting And Public Policy*, *28*(4), 301-327. [online] http://dx.doi.org/10.1016/j.jaccpubpol.2009.06.006

IIA, (2009). *THE ROLE OF INTERNAL AUDITING IN ENTERPRISE-WIDE RISK MANAGEMENT*. *Na.theiia.org*.

Laisasikorn, K. & Rompho, N. (2014). A Study of the Relationship Between a Successful Enterprise Risk Management System, a Performance Measurement System and the Financial Performance of Thai Listed Companies. *Journal Of Applied Business And Economics*, *16*(2), 81-92.

Lynall, M., Golden, B., & Hillman, A. (2003). BOARD COMPOSITION FROM ADOLESCENCE TO MATURITY: A MULTITHEORETIC VIEW. *Academy Of Management Review*, *28*(3), 416-431. [online] http://dx.doi.org/10.5465/amr.2003.10196743

McShane, M., Nair, A., & Rustambekov, E. (2011). Does Enterprise Risk Management Increase Firm Value?. *Journal Of Accounting, Auditing & Finance*, *26*(4), 641-658. [online] http://dx.doi.org/10.1177/0148558x11409160

Nocco, B. & Stulz, R. (2006). Enterprise Risk Management: Theory and Practice. *Journal Of Applied Corporate Finance*, *18*(4), 8-20. [online] http://dx.doi.org/10.1111/j.1745-6622.2006.00106.x

Paape, L. & Speklé, R. (2012). The Adoption and Design of Enterprise Risk Management Practices: An Empirical Study. *European Accounting Review*, 1-32. [online] http://dx.doi.org/10.1080/09638180.2012.661937

Pagach, D. & Warr, R. (2010). The Characteristics of Firms That Hire Chief Risk Officers. *Journal Of Risk And Insurance*, *78*(1), 185-211.

RIMS, (2007). *RIMS Risk Maturity Model (RMM) for Enterprise Risk Management*. *www.logicmanager.com*. [online] http://www.logicmanager.com/pdf/rims_rmm_executive_summary.pdf

Togok, S., bt Isa, C., & Zainuddin, S. (2014). Review of Enterprise Risk Management (ERM) Literature. In *International Conference on Technology and Business Management*. American University in the Emirates, Dubai. [online] http://eprints.um.edu.my/13412/1/D4140-Final.pdf

Woods, M. (2009). A contingency theory perspective on the risk management control system within Birmingham City Council. *Management Accounting Research*, *20*(1), 69-81. [online] http://dx.doi.org/10.1016/j.mar.2008.10.003

Zhao, X., Hwang, B., & Pheng Low, S. (2014). Enterprise risk management implementation in construction firms. *Management Decision*, *52*(5), 814-833. [online] http://dx.doi.org/10.1108/md-02-2014-0082

CHAPTER 7

FINANCIAL STOCK MARKETS' REACTION TO TERRORISM ACTIVITIES

Summary of Chapter Seven

This chapter explains the impact of terrorism activities on different (developing and developed) economies' financial stock markets. Spain, the United Kingdom, India, Pakistan, America, and France were chosen for the analysis. The variables considered were terrorist activities and market returns of the financial stock markets. Daily time series data for the period from 2001 to 2018 was analyzed by applying a linear regression model to estimate the effects of terrorist activities on the financial stock market returns of developed and developing countries. The results suggest that the market return is affected by terror events and overall, the model is statistically significant. The significant influence of terrorist activities on financial market returns offers financial markets' stakeholders not only an understanding of the direction of market swing following terror factors on stock market, but also offers guidance towards investment decision-making and timing. The study further discussed the way terrorism activities influence the overall market return.

Keywords: Terrorism Activities, Financial Stock Market, Linear Regression Model, Quantitative Analysis, Deductive Approach

Section 1: Chapter introduction

Change in economic circumstances affects the stock prices, which will have a direct reflection on the discounted value of the existing and future performance of the firm. Literature discusses that positive and negative changes in the stock prices can possibly be connected to events; see Schwert (1981) and Freytag et al. (2009). The benefit of the event study method lies in its inherent ability to make out such untoward changes, as its basis lies in the overall assessment of investors who have at their hands such means as to be able to assess individual firms' market value. Investors can easily, inexpensively, and quickly, change their decisions about buying and selling stocks. Whenever information about a military attack or some terrorist activity is reported, which in itself results in great upheavals and disturbances, it causes someone who has invested capital in those places to try to leave the area, along with their capital, immediately. The term 'terrorism' has been defined by different researchers, but Sandler and Enders (2008) describe terrorism as the premeditated, threatened, or actual use of force or violence to achieve a political goal through fear, coercion, or intimidation. This definition brings within its fold the four features of terrorist activity as given by Shughart (2006): firstly, using violence for political purpose; secondly, a well-devised way for action; thirdly, such behavior which is not within the accepted rules of warfare; and fourthly, an effort to provoke great fear and a sense of insecurity among the people, particularly civilians.

Terrorism causes the biggest threat to the economy. The greatest of them all is the loss of human life, and in particular the lives of innocent people. A right-minded person would never commit such a heinous crime. Then, the psychological aspect of these atrocious acts in the minds of the public cannot be overemphasized. According to Tavares (2004) and Crain and Crain (2006), these terrorist acts cause a disruption of the economy, and slow down progress. Foreign investors hesitate to invest in such adverse circumstances (Abadie and Gardeazabal 2008). Without doubt, terrorism has now become a major security issue in the world today. With increases in these events, governments consider counter-terrorism measures as a priority of their agendas. As a result, most governments react to limit individual freedoms and civil rights, but they also increase the portion of anti-terrorist spending in their budget. According to a report issued by the United Kingdom's security service, MI5, the total annual expenditure on anti-terror activities and intelligence was scheduled to rise from £2.5 billion in 2007/08 to £3.5 billion by 2010/11. The aim of the present study is to analyze the impact of terrorist attacks on the financial markets, and the response of the markets after the occurrence of such threatened events.

The motivation behind writing this chapter is to understand the stock markets of different developing and developed nations, and how these economies are badly affected by terrorist activities. Terror attacks can inflict heart-breaking damage to human life, and destruction of property. Now it is a bare truth that these losses are not confined to human loss, but disastrous results affect the overall economy. Financial stock markets respond to these activities, and fluctuations in the markets are so visible that they can change the minds of foreign and local investors. The financial markets play a vital role in the development of an economy. Confidence of investors in markets is badly shaken due to terror attacks, and decreased levels of confidence of foreign and local investors will lead to adverse movement of the markets. So this chapter determines the market reaction to terror attacks, and what the measures that investors and policymakers should take to remain stable in such conditions are.

Section 2: Theoretical support/ Literature review

2.1. Theoretical foundation of rational criminal theory

Becker (1968) developed a 'rational criminal' theory, stating that all individuals spend their time in a rational way; that is, a method through which they can maximize their utility between legal and criminal activities. According to his theory, each individual considers the following things before committing a crime: (a) risk of being caught, the chances, and magnitude of the punishment; (b) the stigma and moral cost related with the criminal activities. Becker concluded that a person who is getting the maximum marginal benefit from the criminal activity is more likely to indulge in it. All the evidence stated that an ill-educated person with a lower wage is more likely to perform property crime, rather than murder and other violations that are unconcerned with a person's economic activity.

2.2. Reasons for terrorism-spreading activities

Krueger and Malečková (2003) conducted a study to analyze whether poverty and low education have any contribution to the promotion of terrorist activities. Berrebi (2007) conducted the same study to investigate the correspondence between terrorism, education, and income level, and he concluded that remarkably, being married decreases the chances of involvement in terrorist activities. De Mesquita (2005) demonstrated these findings by presenting a model of the interdependence between terrorist activities, government, and terrorist volunteers, and he concluded that terrorist volunteers are not ill-educated, but that an absence of economic opportunity has a positive relation with terrorism. The study described the roles of ethnic conflict, freedom of speech, political freedom, and economic organizations, in promoting transnational terrorism in the origin countries. It concluded that there is proof that political rights, freedom of speech, of groups, and constitutional elections, can decrease the effects of ethnic terrorism, while economic opportunity can also decrease the chances of terrorist activities. Freytag et al. (2009) demonstrated the role of socio-economic factors in terrorism. They noted that socio-economic situations affect terrorist activities through the opportunity cost of terrorism.

2.3. The economic cost of terrorist activities

Tavares (2004) conducted precise and organized research to find the economic cost of terror incidents at country level. The study assumed that effect of terror attacks on GDP is quantifiable, and comparing it with other aggregate shocks allows the measurement of the cost of terrorism. Lenain et al. (2002 demonstrate the three possible ways through which terror might influence macro-economic activity. Firstly, the decline in insurance coverage can be observed, and is an indication of the increased risk, and greater trading costs that lead toward lesser dealing in international trade and higher defense and security expenditure.

Economic consequences: Hillman (2007) examined and refined arguments about supreme values in rent-seeking economies, likewise in Arab oil-exporting countries, and in the radical Muslim Gaza Strip. The researchers concluded that expected economic prosperity has no impact on the emergence of terror and political violence. Freytag et al. (2009 conducted a study to find the relation between terrorism and socio-economic conditions. The analysis showed an interesting picture. Unexpectedly, the impact of GDP per capita has a positive association with terror activities (besides European countries) in simple form, while the relation converts into a negative when GDP per capita is in quadratic form. The affiliation between investment and terror incidents is extremely negative, excluding Islamic countries where this association is positive. Similarly, the human capital is significantly negatively associated with terrorism activities, excluding Islamic countries.

Benmelech and Berrebi (2007) conducted a study to find the association between human capital of the suicide bombers and the results of their suicide attacks. In the proposed study, they confirm that human capital is a crucial factor in promoting suicide terrorism. The empirical analysis was done by using a regression model, and they concluded that suicide attacks in Israel have a positive association with both standard of living and education.

2.4. Terrorism in developing and developed economies

Hobijn (2002) conducted a study to compare the historical and expected expenses of national security by local governments, and federal and other projects that are conducted by the government. In his study, he addresses three basic questions, starting with the amount that the government will have to spend on security issues. He seeks to answer this question by comparing the historical and expected expenditure of the federal and local government on security issues with expenditure on the other programs. He analyzed that after the disastrous events of September 2001, the US government and private sectors adopted extra security measures, and the cost of carrying out these measures has increased expenditure which has had a great impact on the economic conditions of the country concerned. Moreover, a small change was found in the productivity of labor. Lenain et al. (2002) evaluated that an increased level of terrorist activity has forced governments to spend more on homeland security and on military operations; this phenomenon has been observed more in the US, while to a lesser extent in OECD countries.

2.5. Reasons for increase in terrorist activities

In a recent study, Krueger and Maleckova (2002) examined the major causes of terrorism by using micro data. Public opinion was accessed through different surveys, and they found that the West Bank and Gaza supported the terror attacks being conducted in Israel. Exceptionally, they uncovered the fact that these violent attacks were not at all associated with ill-education or economic status. Another study, describing the features of the terrorist individual, demonstrated that higher income and better education does not lead to lower terrorism activities.

Most of the studies regarding the incidences and causes of terrorism have been performed globally. Blomberg et al. (2004), executed a research which had two linked aspects. Initially, they established and developed a theoretical model to find the link between economic conditions and terror activity. On the other hand, to consider the model, they organized and collected cross country data. Finally, they concluded that states which are entangled in the recession (one phase of the trade cycle) would face an increased number of terror incidents. The intensity of terror shocks varies from group to group, and state to state, as the people have different states of mind, and may be dissatisfied by the political situation, while those lacking the constitutional means are more inclined to perform such attacks. By demonstrating multiple equilibria, the model concluded with two likely outcomes; decreased economic activity will lead to increased terrorist activity, and economic prosperity will lead to decreased terror attacks.

2.6. The influence of terrorist activities on financial stock markets

Neumayer (2004) conducted a study with the objective of analyzing effective policies and other regulatory outcomes to safeguard financial markets from terror attacks. They collected data from New York (in 2001) and Madrid (in 2004) on all the terror activities that occurred in those countries. Their results demonstrated that expanded, sound and liquid markets (incorporating the contingency plans from the viewpoint of business) are more effective and efficient at absorbing the shocks of terror attacks. In any case, the paper clearly shows the responses of the crisis management authorities, and analyzes the effectiveness of these responses and the way these responses affect the financial markets and help them to absorb the shocks, to some extent. Further, they concluded that the primary function of a state bank as lender of the last resort was very effective in controlling the aftermath panic from the market after terror activity.

2.6.1. Terror activities' influence on the Pakistan stock market

Aslam et al. (2015) conducted a study to investigate the connection between terror activities and the response of the financial stock markets, and how these terror shocks affect the development of the financial markets. They selected Pakistan as their sample for this case study because terrorism is increasing day by day in Pakistan, and the country is playing a major role in the war against terrorism. The objective of the paper was to dissect the effects of terrorism on the development of the stock markets of Pakistan, because the performance of the stock exchange represents the economic health and performance of an economy. By utilizing terrorism impact factors, an interesting unique score was developed for the research paper, and a deeper understanding was gained through which to analyze the linkage between the terror shocks and the Karachi Stock Exchange (KSE) index. Moreover, the researchers examined the quantitative significance of selected terror attacks on the KSE. The empirics of the study concluded that while considering the long-term effect of terror activities, financial markets respond in a negative manner, whereas, in the short run, no significant relationship is seen between terrorism and stock return. The results clearly indicated that terror shocks definitely change the investors' states of mind and moods to a large extent, and ultimately, this shifts the economic situation of the country. Therefore, it is right to say that terror represents a prominent setback in the development and health of the economy.

2.6.2. Terror activities' influence on Spain's stock market

Neumayer's detailed study (2004) attempts to analyze the movement of the global financial stock markets. The study chose two main terror attacks to examine the response of the authorities. The first one was the disastrous events of 9/11, and the second was the events of 11 March 2004 in Madrid (Spain). The study argued that flexible, timely and precise reactions of the authorities are important to allow the global financial markets to be efficient in managing the effects of these terror attacks. Due to globalization, the reactions of the authorities and joint efforts between prosecuting and intelligence agencies, financial markets, regulators, and governments, are crucial to develop the financial systems' strength against these terrorist attacks. Different studies have not provided any clue that terrorist activities have a negative effect on stock markets, because the financial markets are more flexible and efficient in other countries, so that they can incorporate the impact of terror activities into their returns.

2.6.3. Terror activities' influence on the United Kingdom stock market

Previous studies on the magnitude and time period of response of the market indices to terrorist attacks examined the impact of attacks on Berlin (2016), New York (2001), NYSE (2016), Madrid (2004), Brussels (2016), London (2005), Paris (2015) and Boston (2013) on the stock exchange indices of the Euronext Index (BEL), USA (S&P), France (CAC), Japan (NIKKEI), UK (FTSE), Spain (IBEX) and Germany (DAX). They used event study methodology and graphical analysis and their results showed that both the time period and magnitude of the terror event have a moderate effect, which reduced over years. They concluded that the selected events have a short term and relatively smaller impact on the financial markets. Whenever new information about an assault circulates in the market it definitely leads toward contagion and uncertainty, and an immediate decline in stock prices. Their results are in accordance with the results of other researchers like Enders and Sandler (2007).

2.6.4. Terror activities' influence on the Indian Stock Market

Aslam et al. (2015) analyzed the effect of 410 terror attacks on the development of five Asian stock exchanges possessing a developed stock exchange and also having a larger number of comparatively intense terrorist incidents. They collected the data into two datasets from the five Asian countries; Bangladesh, India, Indonesia, the Philippines, and Sri Lanka. In this study, 410 terror events were considered from January 1997 to

December 2011. The study used a regression model to calculate the effects of these terror events. The empirical results clearly indicated that stock markets have been significantly affected by terror events. The magnitude of these effects was different with respect to target and country type. The PSEI, DSE and JKSE performed in a negative manner after the terror incident. Attacks in Sri Lanka and Bangladesh significantly affected the CSE and DSEG indices. In terms of attack type, bomb blasts and suicide attacks had a particularly negative effect on DSEG and CSE on the second day of attack. Further analysis brings to light that those attacks which target the business sector and defense/security forces, negatively knock the returns of Asian stock exchanges. Likewise, the more austere the terror attack (i.e., more injuries and fatalities), the greater the negative impact on the returns of stock market.

2.6.5. Terror activities' influence on France's stock market

Chesney et al. (2010) examined analytically the effect of terrorism shocks on the behavior of commodity markets, bonds, and stock markets. In this study they used two types of dataset. In the first, the prices of daily stock market indices were collected. They gathered the data of daily stock prices from Data Stream and for each index they considered the daily prices encompassing the period between 4 January 1994 and 16 September 2005. The selected prices include 3054 data points. Then they calculated the logarithm of the percentage index return. For this study they gathered data on terror incidents which happened in 25 countries over a period of 11 years. To get the results they used a filtered GARCH approach, event study methodology, and non-parametric methods on the data.

2.6.6. Terror activities' influence on the US stock market

Lacker (2004) stated that many key market elements were damaged or destroyed in the attacks which affected significant operations surrounding the World Trade Center, causing a widespread closure of the New York financial markets and a great loss of human life. Over 74% of the total of civilian casualties were in the World Trade Center. The government and the local securities markets were largely and badly affected, with of the loss of small brokers, as well as the largest interdealer broker, Cantor Fitzgerald whose offices were situated in the Center. Previous studies have shown that when the securities and payment transactions are done through manual processing, it significantly delays the clearing and settlement procedures, which also raises uncertainty among traders as to whether their ongoing trades will complete or not. Chen and Siems (2004) used event study methodology to capture the impact of fourteen terror attacks dating back to 1915. In addition to the selected 14 events, the researchers also encompassed the attacks of Iraq on Kuwait and the 9/11 attacks on the World Trade Center and the Pentagon.

Section 3: Methodologies and approaches

3.1. Data

The methodology section explains the dataset used to be analyzed. There are various methods and approaches used by this study. Firstly, the researcher utilized the deductive method approach as it is based on hypothesis testing. The data regarding terror activity was taken from the Global Terrorism Index.[1] To calculate the daily average return, this study collected the opening and closing indexes of the selected stock markets. 'Financial markets' is a broad-ranging term that covers all marketplaces where equities, currencies, derivatives, and bonds, are traded by buyers and sellers. So, the population of this study includes big global stock markets as well as small financial ones. The sample of study includes five stock market indices which include Spain, the United Kingdom, Pakistan, India, France, and the United States of America. Data from these countries was collected from the New York Stock Exchange, Bolsa de Madrid (Spain), the London Stock Exchange, the Karachi Stock Exchange, the Bombay Stock Exchange and France's Stock Exchange. The study is based on the sample of six countries, four of which are developed countries and the remaining two countries are developing countries. For the developed countries, this study collected samples from Spain, the US, France, and the United Kingdom. All these countries are high in human development with high income levels. To examine the effect of terrorism on the South Asian region, we selected the Maldives, Pakistan, and India as these countries are most affected by terror events. The data of this study was collected from the Global Terrorism Database and the data of the exogenous variable (market return) was collected from Yahoo Finance.

---

[1] The Global Terrorism Database (GTD) was started in 2001 at the University of Maryland. The complete information and data was gathered by the Pinkerton Global Intelligence Services (PGIS). The general public can freely and openly access this database and gather information about terrorist attacks. The National Consortium established for the Study of Terrorism and Responses to Terrorism (START) designed the GTD so that people can collect the information through the internet and all the information can be assessed in a short time.

3.2. Statistics

Regression analyses were used to analyze the impact of terror incidents on financial stock markets, and to estimate the results, time series EViews econometric software was used. In this study regression analysis was used because researchers such as Berrebi (2007), Freytag et al. (2009,) and Neumayer (2004) also used the same unit to analyze the impact of terror attack on financial markets. Data is time series in nature and was collected from 1 January 2001 to 31 December 2018. The econometrics model of study is:

Market Return = α + ß (Terrorism Activities) + μ

Where; Y = Dependent variable (Market Return); α = intercept of the regression model; ß = Regression coefficient; X = independent variable and μ = Disturbance term of the regression

Section 4: Empirical Analysis of Terror Activities' Influence

4.1. Test of heteroskedasticity

The Breusch-Pagan-Godfrey test was used to test the heteroskedasticity of data, as this measure is most commonly used. We have developed the following hypotheses: Null hypothesis: residuals are homoskedastic; and Alternative hypothesis: residuals are heteroskedastic.

Table-1 Test of heteroskedasticity.

Models	India (Bombay Stock Exchange)	Spain (Bolsa de Madrid)	Pakistan (Karachi Stock Exchange)	France (France Stock Exchange)	USA (New York Stock Exchange)	UK (London Stock Exchange)
P-value	0.180	0.244	0.640	0.947	0.108	0.130
F-statistics	5.343	4.663	0.218	3.063	4.788	4.711

Source: Developed by researcher (2020)

Bombay Stock Exchange (India) results: F-Statistics shows that the overall model is significant in nature (Table 1). The observed P-value is 18%, which is greater than 5%, which means the residuals of the model are homoskedastic. So, we accept the null hypothesis and reject the alternative hypothesis.

Bolsa de Madrid (Spain) results: F-Statistics shows that the overall model is significant in nature (Table 1). The observed P-value is 24%, which is greater than 5%, which means the residuals of the model are homoskedastic. So, we accept the null hypothesis and reject the alternative hypothesis.

Karachi Stock Exchange (Pakistan) results: The Karachi Stock exchange was selected to analyze the impact of terror activities on the stock market of Pakistan (Table 1). The P-value is 64%, which is greater than 5%, which clearly shows that the model is free from heteroskedasticity. Homoskedasticity exists in the model and it is also desirable to have it. So, we reject the alternative hypothesis and accept the null hypothesis.

France's Stock Exchange (CAC 40 France) results: In this study to analyze the impact of terror activities on the financial markets of France we selected the CAC 40 index, as the CAC 40 is a benchmark French stock market index (Table 1). Results show that the P-value is 94%. That is clearly greater than 5%. The results of the Bruesch Pagan test clearly mentioned that the model is free from heteroskedasticity. So, we fail to reject null hypothesis and accept it.

New York Stock Exchange (US) results): The New York Stock Exchange is among the largest stock exchanges of the world in accordance with its market capitalization (Table 1). The results of the Bruesch Pagan Godfrey test reveal that the model is homoskedastic and the residuals are free from heteroskedasticity, because the P-value (10.8%) is greater than the standard value of 5%. So we reject the alternative hypothesis and accept the null hypothesis.

London Stock Exchange (UK) results: The London Stock Exchange is the primary stock exchange of the United Kingdom (Table 1). In this research, the opening and closing prices of the 100 index of the London Stock Exchange was collected from Yahoo Finance. The results of the Bruesch Pagan test reveal that the model is free from heteroskedasticity and homoskedasticity exists. As the P-value of 13% is greater than 5%, we fail to reject null hypothesis and conclude that residuals are free from the heteroskedasticity problem.

4.2. Regression model

The table below shows the results of the autoregressive regression model, as the dependent variable has appeared as an independent variable in the model.

Table-2: Regression Model

Regression Model Least Square

Observation: 4481 after adjustment

Sample: 2001 to 2018

Dependent Variable: Market Return

Models	**India**			**Spain**			**Pakistan**		
	t-statistics	**P-value**	**R^2**	**t-statistics**	**P-value**	**R^2**	**t-statistics**	**P-value**	**R^2**
	-52.81	0.023	0.63	-11.30	0.002	0.62	-10.50	0.038	0.64
Models	France			USA			UK		
	t-statistics	P-value	R^2	t-statistics	P-value	R^2	t-statistics	P-value	R^2
	-8.268	0.026	0.68	-16.09	0.000	0.69	-19.26	0.000	0.81

Source: Developed by researcher (2020)

India's regression results: The value of R^2 represents that a 63% variation in the dependent variable is due to change in the independent variable (Table 2). The remaining 39% variation in the dependent variable is due to other factors. Secondly, the independent variable of the model is individually significantly influencing the dependent variable (market return). The T-Statistics value is -52.81 which shows that there is negative influence of terror activities on stock return. The P-value against the independent variable (terror activity) is 2.36%, which is less than 5%. This shows that terror activity is a negative and significant (independent variable) influence on the dependent variable that is market return.

Spain's regression results: The R^2 value is 62%. That shows the variation in the dependent variable due to the independent variable (Table 2). Here, the variation in the dependent variable is 62% which comes from terrorist activities, while the remaining 38% is due to other factors. Secondly, terrorist activities are individually significantly influencing the market return, as the P-value is less than 5%.

France's regression results: In this regression mode, the value of R^2 is 68.70% which shows that the model is best fitted and we can say that 68.70% change in the dependent variable is coming from the change in independent variable (Table 2). Secondly, the P-value is 2.420%, which is less than 5%, which shows that the terrorism activities, which are the independent variable of this study, are significantly affecting the market return.

Pakistan's regression results: The R^2 value is 64%. This shows the variation in the dependent variable due to the independent variable. Here the variation in dependent variable is 64% which comes from terrorist activity, while the remaining 36% is due to other factors. Secondly, terrorist activities are individually significantly influencing the market return, as the P-value is less than 5%.

US' regression results: The regression model shows that terror activities are individually significant in affecting the market response. The corresponding P-value against the terror activities is less than 5% which clearly assures the significance of the independent variable. Secondly, the model contains a good R2 figure of 69%, which is greater than 60%, so it clearly demonstrates the good fit of the model. This R2 means that 69% variation in the market return is due to terror activities in the state.

UK's regression results: In the above table, the regression analysis shows that the model is a good fit, as the value of R^2 is 81.477% which is more than 60%. The value of R^2 shows that the 81.477% variation in the dependent variable (market return) is coming from the independent variable (terror activity). Secondly, the independent variable of the model is individually significant, as terror activities are significantly affecting the market return, because the P-value against the terror activities is less than 5%.

Section 5: Chapter conclusion

This chapter examined how terror activities influence the stock returns of different economies. We have discussed the results of studies in different stock exchange contexts. The Bolsa de Madrid results are aligned with Neumayer's (2004) study. The results of this study show that Spain is badly affected by terror attacks. The results of the OLS Regression model suggest that the Bolsa de Madrid Stock Exchange is adversely affected by terror activities in the country. The Value of R^2 represents that 62% variation in the market return is due to national and international terror activities. This finding shows that when terrorism occurs it always affect the minds of investors and ultimately decreases market return. The Karachi Stock Exchange (KSE) results are aligned with Alam's (2012) study. Terrorist attacks have a rigorously bad impact on the stability of financial stocks. Due to such shocks, investment, and especially foreign investment, is reduced. This means that as terror attacks increase, the financial stability and performance of the Karachi Stock Exchange will decline. We can conclude that terrorism has a negative relation with the market return. The 64% variation in the market return is due to terror activity, and the remaining variation in the market return of the Karachi Stock Exchange is due to other various factors, such as political and economic instability, etc., that are not included in the current study. The Bombay Stock Exchange results are aligned with Aslam et al.'s (2015) study. The market return of the Bombay Stock Exchange is badly affected by terror attacks. The coefficient of the simple regression model is – 0.44, which shows that a one-unit increase in terror activity will lead to a decrease in market return by 0.44%. This clearly indicates that the Bombay Stock Exchange is experiencing an adverse impact from terrorist activities in India. A large number of terrorist activities affect the economy of India, and its general and financial markets in particular. The France CAC 40 Stock Exchange Index results are aligned with Berrebi's (2007) study. Terrorism cannot present fruitful results to any nation, and the same is true with France. Fewer terrorist activities occur in

France, but when they do occur, it always affects the minds of investors, and ultimately decreases the market return. The results of the OLS regression model suggest that France's CAC 40 Stock Exchange is adversely affected by terror activities in the country. The value of R^2 shows that 68% variation in market return is due to national and international terror activities. The London Stock Exchange (LSE) results are aligned with Berrebi (2007). OLSrRegression analysis suggests that the LSE is least affected by terror activities, because due to high levels of security, the country faces fewer terror shocks. The coefficient of the model is -0.018 which shows a small change in the market return is due to terror activity. However, the market is getting a negative impact from terror shocks. There are also other factors that affect the market return of the London Stock Exchange, such as the political situation. The New York Stock Exchange (NYSE) results are aligned with Neumayer's (2004) study. The results of the regression model suggest that the return of the New York Stock Exchange is negatively related to terror activities. The coefficient of the regression model represents that a one unit increase in terror activity will lead to a decrease in market return of 0.65%.

5.1. Concluding remarks

This chapter analyzed the impact of international and local terror activities on the financial markets of Spain, the UK, the US, France, Pakistan, and India, by using time series data from 2001 to 2018. By using OLS regression analyses, this study analyzed that terrorist attacks can badly impact the economic and financial situation of a country. The decline in the stock markets clearly shows that beyond the personal injury and loss of life of victims, terrorism has a real economic cost that decreases firms' profits.

5.2. Implication and recommendations for study

Through this analysis, people can generate policies and managerial implications for national security, security trades, and portfolio allocation. By considering the activities of terrorists, people can manage their portfolios to minimize the effects of these shocks, as the study demonstrates that the impact of these terror shocks is adverse on the markets. So, in the light of these findings, investors can manage the holding periods of their investments. Anti-terrorism policies should be redesigned to cope with terrorist attacks.

References

Alam, A. (2012). Terrorism and stock market development: causality evidence from Pakistan. *Journal of Financial Crime*, *20*(1), 116-128.

Abadie, A. and J. Gardeazabal, 2008. Terrorism and the world economy. European Economic Review, 52(1): 1-27.

Aslam, F., H.G. Kang, W. Mohti, A. Rafique and A. SALMAN, 2015. The impact of terrorism on financial markets: Evidence from Asia. The Singapore Economic Review: 1550111, 63(5), 1183-1204.

Basuchoudhary, A. and W.F. Shughart, 2010. On ethnic conflict and the origins of transnational terrorism. Defence and Peace Economics, 21(1): 65-87.Available at: https://doi.org/10.1080/10242690902868343.

Becker, G.S., 1968. Crime and punishment: An economic approach. In The economic dimensions of crime. London: Palgrave Macmillan. pp: 13-68.

Benmelech, E. and C. Berrebi, 2007. Human capital and the productivity of suicide bombers. Journal of Economic Perspectives, 21(3): 223-238.Available at: https://doi.org/10.1257/jep.21.3.223.

Berrebi, C., 2007. Evidence about the link between education, poverty and terrorism among palestinians. Peace Economics, Peace Science, and Public Policy, 13(1): 1-38.Available at: https://doi.org/10.2202/1554-8597.1101.

Blomberg, S.B., G.D. Hess and A. Orphanides, 2004. The macroeconomic consequences of terrorism. Journal of Monetary Economics, 51(5): 1007-1032.

Chen, A.H. and T.F. Siems, 2004. The effects of terrorism on global capital markets. European Journal of Political Economy, 20(2): 349-366. Available at: https://doi.org/10.1016/s0176-2680(03)00102-2.

Chesney, M., G. Reshetar and M. Karaman, 2010. The impact of terrorism on financial markets: An empirical study. Journal of Banking & Finance, 35(2): 253-267.

Crain, N.V. and W.M. Crain, 2006. Terrorized economies. Public Choice, 128(1-2): 317-349.Available at: https://doi.org/10.1007/s11127-006-9056-6.

De Mesquita, E.B., 2005. The quality of terror. American Journal of Political Science, 49(3): 515-530.

Economic Consequences of Terrorism in Developed and Developing Countries: An Overview. Terrorism, Economic Development, and Political Openness. P. Keefer and N. Loayza, Cambridge University Press: New York: 17-47.

Freytag, A., J.J. Krüger, D. Meierrieks and F.G. Schneider, 2009. The origins of terrorism cross-country estimates on socio-economic determinants of terrorism (No. 2009, 009). Jena Economic Research Papers from Friedrich-Schiller-University Jena

Hillman, A.L., 2007. Economic and security consequences of supreme values. Public Choice, 131(3-4): 259-280.Available at: https://doi.org/10.1007/s11127-007-9167-8.

Hobijn, B., 2002. What will homeland security cost? Federal Reserve Bank of New York, Economic Policy Review, Volume 8, Number 2.

Krueger, A.B. and J. Maleckova, 2002. Education, poverty, political violence and terrorism: Is there a causal connection? National Bureau of Economic Research (No. w9074).

Krueger, A.B. and J. Malečková, 2003. Education, poverty and terrorism: Is there a causal connection? Journal of Economic Perspectives, 17(4): 119-144.Available at: https://doi.org/10.1257/089533003772034925.

Lacker, J.M., 2004. Payment system disruptions and the federal reserve following september 11, 2001. Journal of Monetary Economics, 51(5): 935-965.Available at: https://doi.org/10.1016/j.jmoneco.2004.04.005.

Lenain, P., M. Bonturi and V. Koen, 2002. The economic consequences of terrorism. OECD Working Paper. OECD Economics Department Working Papers from OECD Publishing, No334

Neumayer, E., 2004. The impact of political violence on tourism: Dynamic cross-national estimation. Journal of Conflict Resolution, 48(2): 259-281.Available at: https://doi.org/10.1177/0022002703262358.

Sandler, T. and W. Enders, 2008. Economic consequences of terrorism in developed and developing countries. Terrorism, Economic Development, and Political Openness, pp 17-47.

Schwert, G.W., 1981. Using financial data to measure effects of regulation. The Journal of Law and Economics, 24(1): 121-158.Available at: https://doi.org/10.1086/466977.

Shughart, W.F., 2006. An analytical history of terrorism, 1945–2000. Public Choice, 128(1-2): 7-39.Available at: https://doi.org/10.1007/s11127-006-9043-y.

Tavares, J., 2004. The open society assesses its enemies: Shocks, disasters and terrorist attacks. Journal of Monetary Economics, 51(5): 1039-1070. Available at: https://doi.org/10.1016/j.jmoneco.2004.05.003.

CHAPTER 8

INCREASING TRUST IN E-COMMERCE DURING THE COVID-19 PANDEMIC

Summary of Chapter Eight

The explosion of e-commerce activities required academia and industry to recognize the key factors affecting customer online repurchase intention. The purpose of writing this chapter is to determine the primary drivers of customer repeat-purchase intention with regard to trust and inertia. The chapter proposes an integrated model of online repeat-purchase intention. With the prevalence of the internet, there is an interactive relationship built between consumers and online channels, and now much attention is paid to this by practitioners and researchers. In e-commerce, online shopping is available through the internet, and online shoppers' repeat purchase intention is influenced by many factors, such as consumer inertia and online trust. Managers and academics know little about how the collective effect of consumer inertia and online trust influences repeat-purchase intention. Based on the perspective of Theory of Reasoned Action (TRA) and the Push and Pull Mooring (PPM) Model, the aim of writing this chapter is to explore the relationship between consumer inertia, online trust, and repeat-purchase intention in the e-commerce world. This study found a result which is somewhat consistent with the literature. Overall, it is concluded that consumer inertia and online trust has a significant impact on consumer repeat purchase intention. Along with this, the study suggests that alternative attraction moderates this relationship. The findings of this research will enable website operators to manage different strategies to attract and maintain online customers. Limitations, practical implications and future direction are provided at the end of this study.

Keywords - Online Trust, Consumer Inertia, Repeat-Purchase Intention, Alternative Attraction, E-Commerce

Section 1: Introduction

E-commerce websites have changed the way consumers purchase, and e-commerce has become a new medium for retail businesses. Gradually, more consumers have begun to purchase products and services from e-commerce websites instead of going to a physical store. Online shopping offers unique advantages compared to traditional face-to-face mode of commerce, such as increased availability, extensive selection, and many more. E-retailers face competition in the market due to increasing numbers of online shopping websites. In Pakistan, competition has increased at a remarkable rate over the last couple of years as different online websites are launched, such as Daraz.pk, iShopping.pk, Kaymu, etc. Now customers are not tied to one purchase point; their intentions vary, day by day. It is important for e-retailers to maintain customer repurchase intention and sustain operations in order to gain competitive advantage in the market·[1] A number of studies have argued that the most important factor in online shoppers repeat purchase intention is online trust.[2] [3] Inertia helps the consumer to avoid dealing with unknown and unfamiliar providers. Where a high level of inertia exists, customers stick to their current service providers, which leads them to make the decision to repeat a purchase.[4] In a competitive business environment, customers may prefer to buy from a store which appears more attractive, so the cost to them of switching is high. This is insignificant in the online shopping context, where a customer can easily switch service provider with just one click of a mouse. For that reason, this study uses the variable of alternative attraction, which negatively moderates the relationship between consumer inertia and repeat purchase intention, as well as the relationship between customer online trust and repeat purchase intention.[1]

The motivation behind this research is that there is a small but growing bank of literature regarding inertia. Consumer inertia and online trust have a tendency to influence the repeat-purchase intention of customers. This study contributes to the literature on consumer inertia, and its effect on repeat purchase intention, by using a larger sample of customers over a significant amount of time. The researcher collected a dataset from 4100 consumers of online shopping websites in 2016. The aim of this research was to investigate the impact of online trust and inertia on customer repeat purchase intentions, in the Pakistani context. The other objective was to analyze whether female online shoppers are more attracted to alternative offers than male online shoppers. Previous studies on online shopping concentrate on consumer trust levels which effect repeat-purchases; very little literature is focused on the significant impact of consumer trust and inertia combined. There are differences between Asian and western online shoppers' attitudes. So, this study will contribute to explore the relationship in a Pakistani context. This study will help online website operators to increase customers' repeat purchases by providing them with good purchase experiences in order to develop online trust and inertia.

The chapter is divided into four headings. The second section will give the literature review which explains the theoretical background and relationship analysis of the factors affecting customers' repeat purchases, and it also explains a dummy gender effect on the relationship. The third section demonstrates the research methodology of the paper, the fourth will give research analysis and findings, and the fifth section finally concludes with short recommendations and practical implications of research.

Section 2: Theoretical background

The Push and Pull Mooring effects model and the Theory of Reasoned Action have been used as a theoretical base for the present study. In 1885, Ravenstein suggested that the migration of humans is influenced by push-pull effects.[5][6] This model explains that the migration of humans is as a result of interaction between a push effect and a pull effect, where the push effect operates from the original point, and the pull effect operates from the place of destination. The PPM model properly identifies factors that cause these pull, push, or mooring effects in human migration, or in any switching process. This study is also supported by the Push and Pull Mooring effect model. Bansal stated that in this model, attractive features of an alternative destination pull the migrant to this destination, referring to studies [8] [9] as examples of human migration research.[7] Another theory which supports this concept is the Theory of Reasoned Action, which influences the attitude of the customer and was developed by Icek Ajzen and Martin Fishbein.[10] Reasoned action is concerned with behavioral intention, which means that all our actions depend on reason. The theory supports that customer behavioral intention is dependent upon the customer's attitude and its subjective norms. This study is also supported by Reasoned Action Theory, which states that our behavior is based on norms and attitudes, and our attitudes or actions are based on reason. When organizations increase their customers' trust levels by providing them with good past experiences, their behavioral intention to repurchase the product will increase.

Relationship analysis

Influence of consumer inertia on repeat-purchase intention

Various researchers have documented inertia as a choice of brand. Basically, it is a form of determination in which customers have a higher level of probability of choosing a product or service with which they have a higher level of familiarity or which they have purchased in the past·[11] Olsen explains that inertia directs the customer to buy a product without much consideration.[12] It inclines the consumer to re-patronize the product. According to Roos, inertia can be regarded as a pull factor, as it pulls the customer to increase repeat purchases.[13] Without inertia, a customer may switch from one service provider to another. Customers who have a high level of inertia automatically remain attached to their current service provider, and make their decision to repurchase in a less conscious manner.[4] Saqib found that there is a positive relationship between consumer inertia and the repeat-purchase intention of consumers.[14] According to Kou, female online shoppers have higher levels of inertia, which ultimately lead them to increase their repeat purchase intention.[1] This study suggests that a direct or positive relationship exists between consumer inertia and repeat purchase intention, and consumer inertia has a greater impact on female online shoppers than male.

H1: The positive impact of consumer inertia on repeat purchase intention has more influence on females, as compared to males.

Influence of online trust on repeat purchase intention

In today's e-commerce transactions, customers follow cognitive paths in order to minimize uncertainty and complexity. An effective shortcut in this context is trust,[15] which is a considerable factor affecting shopping intention.[16] Trust is crucial, not only in traditional shopping environments,[17] but also in the context of online shopping. In online shopping, trust plays a vital role because it increases customers' intentions to buy through the internet, and it also helps the consumer avoid possible opportunist behavior from sellers.[18] According to Planned Behavior Theory, customers may be more willing to buy from online websites which they see as less risky, or in which they have trust. Simply, they may not want to shop from a more risky online store.[19] So when trust increases, perception of risk decreases, and this has a direct or indirect effect on internet shopping.[20] Jarvenpaa suggested that customers' willingness to buy is dependent upon their positive or negative attitude towards online websites.[19] Rodgers & Harris stated that women are less satisfied with the experience of online shopping than men.[21] Therefore, this study suggests that a direct or positive relationship exists between online trust and repeat purchase intention, and female trust levels in online shopping are lower than males'.

H2: The positive impact of online trust on repeat purchase intention has more influence on males, as compare to females

The moderating role of alternative attraction

Customers switch from their previous stores, or are attracted to alternatives when other stores offers them higher quality products at lower prices, or more attractive products.[22] Isaac Newton's 'Law of Inertia' also has marketing implications. Customers will stay with their current service provider or e-retailer as long as no other force compels them to change. If they have high levels of inertia, they will be unwilling to change their current service provider, even though the alternatives are offering them more attractive products.[23] In this highly competitive market, various alternatives are offered by service providers so customers can easily switch to one product to another.[24][25] Alternative attraction may weaken customer repurchase intention based on consumer inertia and online trust and further motivate customers to switch to other more attractive stores.[22] According to Kou, female online shoppers are attracted to different offers offered by various alternatives that will lead to a decrease in their inertia and repeat purchase intention.[1] Therefore, this study proposes that alternative attraction negatively moderates the relationship between online trust and consumer inertia, and female shoppers are more likely to be attracted to alternative attractive offers.

H3: The positive impact of consumer inertia on repeat purchase intention with the negative moderating role of alternative attraction has more influence on females, as compare to males.

H4: The positive impact of online trust on repeat purchase intention with the negative moderating role of alternative attraction has more influence on females, as compare to males.

On the basis of the literature, model, and theory, a framework is developed which shows that the consumer inertia and online trust of customers are independent variables. The repeat purchase intention of the customer is a dependent variable and alternative attraction moderates this relationship.

Figure 1: Theoretical framework

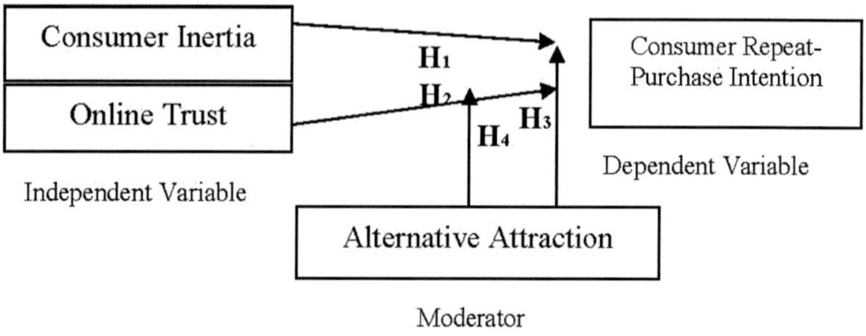

Base article source: Kuo et al. (2013)

Section 3: Approaches/ Methodology

Statistical tools

A quantitative approach was selected for this study to get accurate and reliable results, as, according to Tharenou, this is the appropriate method.[26] Due to time constraints it was not possible to access all online website customers, so a non-probability sampling technique was used with a convenience sampling technique. The advantage of convenience sampling technique is that timely and cost effective data is collected. The customers who were selected as participants of this study were accessible easily, and were willing to take part. Reliability Analysis shows that all items were consistent and reliable in nature. Here, all variable Cronbach's Alpha values were greater than 0.6 which shows that all items were reliable. All variables' skewness and kurtosis values lie between -3 to +3 and -10 to +10 respectively, which shows that data was normally distributed.

Table 1: Demographic profile of sample

Questions	Options	Frequency	Percent
Gender	Male Female	2250 1850	54.9 45.1
Age	Below 20 21-30 31-40 41& Above	1150 1350 920 680	28.0 32.9 22.4 16.5
Family Monthly Income	Under 25000 25000-35000 35000-45000 Above 45000	630 935 971 1564	15.3 22.8 23.6 38.1
Online Website	Daraz.pk Alibaba.com Kaymu.pk Ishopping.pk	1385 585 1288 842	33.7 14.2 31.4 20.5

Source: Developed by researcher (2016)

In this sample, the majority of customers (55%) were male, with 45% being female. Most of the customers belonged to the age group 21-30 years. Most customers (34%) preferred to use the website Daraz.pk, and most respondents (38%) had a family monthly income of above 45,000 which was higher than the others.

Data

The data used in this study was collected from 4100 consumers from the major cities of Pakistan (Rawalpindi, Islamabad, Lahore, Peshawar, Karachi, and Quetta). Ramamurthy stated that a primary data source provides efficient information, and the researcher can then examine new, updated information.[27] Therefore, a primary data collection method was used for this study. The online shoppers (male and female) of Pakistan were the population of this research, so the unit of analysis for this research was the online customer. Those sampled were customers of famous Pakistani online websites, like iShopping.pk, Kaymu.pk, Alibaba.com and Daraz.pk. The collective data was made by combining the datasets from the entire consumer base. Regression analysis was performed on this collective data to find the outcome, which is outlined in the next section. The R-square mean techniques were also used on the dataset.

Section 4: Analysis of Research

Regression analysis

At first, Pearson product moment analysis was conducted to find the two variables' dependency on each other. Sharma stated that the basic purpose of the correlation index is to examine the strength of the relationship between variables.[28]

Table 2: Correlation analysis

Variables	CI	OT	RPI	AA
Consumer Inertia	1			
Online Trust	0.630*	1		
Repeat Purchase Intention	0.684*	0.707*	1	
Alternative Attraction	-0.376*	-0.431*	-0.416*	1

*Correlation is significant at the 0.01 (99%) level, **Correlation is significant at the 0.05 (95%) level, ***Correlation is significant at the 0.10 (90%) level

The correlation between all variables was less than 0.8, which depicts that there was no higher correlation between variables. This means variables act independently, and no issue of co-linearity exists. After examining the relationship through correlation analysis between the variables, regression analysis was conducted to determine the relationship between consumer inertia, online trust and repeat purchase intention, and also to assess the impact of alternative attraction; whether alternative attraction moderates the relationship between independent and dependent variables.

Table 3: Regression analysis

	Un-standardized Coefficient	Standardized Coefficient			
Variables	Beta	Beta	T	Sig	VIF
Constant	0.022		0.362	0.718	
Z score (CI)	0.466	0.466	9.333	0.000	2.048
Z score (OT)	0.336	0.336	6.625	0.000	2.111
Z score (AA)	-0.064	-0.064	-1.609	0.109	1.283
InteractionCI_AA	0.133	0.134	2.983	0.003	1.654
InteractionOT_AA	-0.227	-0.238	-5.273	0.000	1.670
Dummy Gender	-0.109	-0.052	-1.491	0.137	1.012

In this study, the value of the adjusted R-square in Model 1 is .597 which means that a 59% change in repeat purchase intention was because of independent variables, i.e. consumer inertia, and online trust. The value of the adjusted R-square in Model 2 was 0.629, which means that a 62% change in repeat purchase intention was because of independent variables in the presence of alternative attraction (the moderator).

The un-standardized and standardized values of consumer inertia, online trust, and alternative attraction were 0.466, 0.336 and -0.064 respectively. The Beta value of consumer inertia was greater than other variables, which shows that consumer inertia has greater impact on repeat purchase intention than online trust and alternative attraction. Consumer inertia and online trust's significant value was 0.000, which was less than 0.01 ($p<0.01$, sig at 99%). The t-value shows that there is a positive relationship between variables. Hence, H1 and H2 were accepted, as consumer inertia and online trust has positive impact on repeat purchase intention. Un-standardized and standardized value of interaction CI_AA were 0.133 and 0.134 respectively, which shows small impact. The t-value of interaction was 2.983, which was positive, and the significant value was 0.003 which was less than all levels, so alternative attraction has a significant but positive impact on the relationship between consumer inertia and repeat purchase intention. Therefore, hypothesis H3 was rejected because it shows that alternative attraction has a negative impact on the relationship. Un-standardized and standardized values of interaction OT_AA were -0.227 and -0.238 respectively, which shows that alternative attraction has a moderate impact on the relationship. The t-value of interaction was -5.273, which was negative, and the significant value was 0.000, which was less than all levels, so alternative attraction has significant and negative impact on the relationship between online trust and repeat purchase intention. Therefore, hypothesis H4 was accepted because it shows that alternative attraction has negative impact on the relationship. The dummy gender variable significant value was 0.137, which shows that dummy gender was insignificant; there was no impact of dummy gender on relationship.

Section 5: Discussion and Conclusion

Discussion

This chapter explored the relationship between inertia, trust and the repeat purchase intention of customers, and also explained whether alternative attraction moderates the relationship or not. Based on previous frameworks and theories, this study developed a combined model of consumer trust and inertia in the context of internet shopping. The findings and literature of this study provides evidence that a customer's trust and inertia strongly affect his/her perception of repurchase, and increases his/her purchase intention. The literature of the study suggested that gender has effect on this relationship, as Popcorn & Marigold demonstrated that female online shoppers outnumber male, and also asserted that 80% of buying decisions are made or dominated by women. [29] Conversely, Rodgers & Harris claim that women are less satisfied with the experience of online shopping than men. Simply, female trust levels in online shopping are lower than male levels, but the results of this study contradict with literature, as the results reveal that gender has no influence on the consumer inertia, trust, and repeat purchase intention relationship.[21] Whether the customer is male or female has no impact on his or her trust and inertia levels. Lee & Neale found that consumers with high levels of inertia are satisfied with their service providers, have a high level of trust, and may willingly and non-begrudgingly accept the switching cost.[30] Online vendors can be assured that their satisfied and high-inertia consumers will not penalize them by being attracted to alternative offers, or by switching from their current services. Support for this argument also comes from studies of telephone subscribers, which show that customers avoid dealing with unknown service providers because of a perceived risky environment; they do not want to make a mistake, so they stick to one service provider with a high level of inertia.[31] Consistent with these insights, Gefen avers that, in online shopping, trust and inertia play a vital role because they increase customers' intention of internet shopping and help the consumer avoid possible opportunist behavior from sellers.[18]

Literature suggests that alternative attraction negatively moderates the relationship between consumer inertia and repeat purchase, but the results of this study contradict with literature. It revealed that alternative attraction positively moderates this relationship, which means when alternatives are offered to consumers with a high level of inertia, they do not switch from the existing product. Their inertia levels become high when alternatives attract them towards different offers. On the other hand, the literature suggested that alternative attraction negatively moderates the relationship of online trust and repeat purchase intention, and results of the study support this concept that when alternatives are offered to customers they switch from their current service provider. Literature supports the concept that online trust and inertia has a positive impact on repeat purchase intention. The collective findings of this study revealed that without considering the level of consumer trust and inertia, studies may fail to provide a complete picture of consumer repurchasing and switching behavior.

Conclusion

The aim of this chapter was to find the relationship between consumer inertia, online trust, and repeat purchase intention in the e-commerce world. The results of this study are somewhat consistent with the literature. The researcher used primary data for the collection of the questionnaire. The sample of this study was online website users of the major cities of Pakistan (Rawalpindi, Islamabad, Lahore, Peshawar, Karachi, and Quetta). There were four hypotheses, and three were accepted. At the same time, a small but growing literature appears to provide support for these hypotheses. In a nutshell, it is stated that inertia and trust independently affect repeat purchase intention, and alternative attraction positively moderates consumer inertia and negatively moderates the online trust and repeat purchase intention relationship. From a practical standpoint, the study results show that trust and inertia are the strongest predictors of consumer repeat purchase intention. Thus, online retailers should put more emphasis on the consumer trust and inertia relationship. The study results show that online trust and inertia are affected by alternative (competitors') offers, so it is important for online vender to focus on their customers, to make them satisfied through initiatives such as better customer service, taking immediate action on complaints, direct and favorable comparisons with competing brand, and highlighting the advantages that accompany switching costs.

According to our knowledge, many studies have been conducted on trust and inertia, but this study is significantly different from previous studies because of its data variation, i.e. data collected from different cities of Pakistan. The people of different cities had different views regarding online shopping. This study also contributes to the literature on consumer inertia by using a larger sample of 4100 consumers over a significant amount of time. Distinct in this research is the acknowledgment of various factors which affect the repeat purchase intention in different ways. This study is different from other studies because of its contribution to the literature, the selected population, and the variables used, so it is unique in nature. In future, in order to get a deeper understanding of trust formation and customer repeat purchase intention, a more comprehensive model should be developed. In future this model can be extended to include the components of inertia. Since the role of inertia-indifference and inertia-satisfied customers in explaining the customer repeat purchase intention has rarely been studied, it would be a remarkable extension of this research.

References

[1] Kuo Y F, Hu T L., & Yang, S. C. (2013) Effects of inertia and satisfaction in female online shoppers on repeat-purchase intention. Managing Service Quality: An International Journal.168 – 187

[2] Keiningham T L, Cooil B, Aksoy L, Andreassen T, Weiner J (2007) The value of different customer satisfaction and loyalty metrics in predicting customer retention, recommendation, and share-of-wallet. Managing Service Quality, 361-384.

[3] Tsai H T, Huang H C (2007) Determinants of e-repeat-purchase intentions: an integrative model of quadruple retention drivers. Information and Management, 231-239.

[4] Gulati R (1995) Does familiarity breed trust? The implications of repeated ties for contractual choice in alliance. Academy of Management Journal, 85-112.

[5] Ramamurthy G (2011) Research Methodology. New Delhi: Dream Tech Press.

[6] Lee E S (1966) A theory of migration.Demography, 47-57.

[7] Bansal H S, Taylor S F, St James Y (2005) Migrating to new service providers: toward a unifying framework of consumers' switching behaviours. Journal of the Academy of Marketing Science, 96-115.

[8] Dorigo G, Tobler W (1983) Push-Pull Migration Laws. Annals of the Association of American Geographers. 1-17.

[9] Moon B (1995) Paradigms in migration research: exploring 'moorings' as a schema. Progress in Human Geography, 504-24.
[10] Ajzen I, Fishbein M (1980) Theory of Reasoned Action. Relationship of Behavioral Intention to Behavior.
[11] Dube J P, Hitsch G J, Rossi P E (2010) State dependence and alternative explanations for consumer inertia. The RAND Journal of Economics. 417-445
[12] Olsen S (2012) Certainty, risk and knowledge in the satisfaction-purchase intention relationship in a new product experiment. Asia Pacific Journal of Marketing and Logistics.
[13] Roos I (1999) Switching process in customer relationships. Journal of Service Research. 68-85.
[14] Saqib K, Mahmood A, khan M, Hashmi M (2015) Impact of Consumer Inertia on Purchase Intention under the Influence of Subjective Product Knowledge. International Journal of u- and e- Service, Science and Technology. 293-298
[15] Grabner-Kreuter S (2002) The Role of Consumer' trust in online shopping. Journal of Business Ethics. 43-50.
[16] Dennis A C, Jayawardhena B C, papamatthaious E (2010) Antecedents of internet shopping intention and moderating role of substitutability. The International Review Of Retail, Distribution And Consumer Research. 411-430
[17] Bloemer J M M, Odekerken-Schroder G (2002) Store Satisfaction and Store Loyalty Explained By Customer- and Store Related Factors. Journal of Consumer Satisfaction, Dissatisfaction and Complaining Behaviour. 68-80.
[18] Gefen D, Karahanna E, Straub D W (2003) Trust and TAM in online shopping: an integrated model. MIS Quarterly ABI/INFORM, 51.
[19] Jarvenpaa S L, Tractinsky N, Vitale M (2000) Consumer Trust in an internet store. Information Technology and Management, 45-45.
[20] Celik H E, Yilmaz V (2011) Extending the Technology acceptance Model for adoption of E-Shopping By Consumers In Turkey. Journal Of Electronic Commerce Research.
[21] Rodgers S, Harris M A (2003) Gender and E-Commerce: An Exploratory Study. Journal of Advertising Research.
[22] Keaveney S M (1995) Customer switching behavior in service industries: an exploratory study. Journal of Marketing, 71-82.
[23] Liu T C, Wu L W, Hung C T (2007) The effects of inertia and switching barriers on satisfaction-retention relationship: a case of financial service industries. Journal of Management. 671-687.

[24] Bansal H S, Irving P G Taylor S F (2004) A three-component model of customer commitment to service providers. Journal of the Academy of Marketing Science, 234-250.
[25] Jones T O Sasser W E (1995) Why satisfied customers defect. Harvard Business Review. 88-99.
[26] Tharenou P, Donohueis R, Cooper B (2007) Management Research Methods. Press New York: Cambridge University.
[27] Ravenstein E G (1885) The Laws of Migration.Journal of the Statistical Society of London. 167-235
[28] Sharma A (2005) Text Book Of Correlations And Regression. New Delhi: Discovery Publishing House.
[29] Popcorn F, Marigold L (2000) EVEolution: The eight truths of marketing to women. New York: Hyperion.
[30] Lee R, Neale L (2012) Interactions and consequences of inertia and switching costs. Journal of Services Marketing, 26(5). 365 - 374
[31] Miravete E J, Palacios-Huerta (2007) Consumer Inertia, Choice Dependence and Learning from Experience in a Repeated Decision Problem. ICEPR Conference on Applied Industrial Organization in Leuven.